Palgrave Studies in Moral and Mindful Approaches to Leadership and Business

Series Editor
Joan Marques, School of Business, Woodbury University, Burbank, CA, USA

This series aims to infuse greater awareness on the paradigm shift needed in business education and performance. It focuses on mindful approaches to leadership that transcend a bare bottom line focus in business practices. The four main areas on which books will focus are:

- Leadership: within this realm we will be looking for new approaches, or new interpretations to existing approaches. The main aim will be to enrich perspectives on and practices of leadership toward current and future teams, with compassionate and wakeful attention to a wide range of related contemporary topics such as diversity, outsourcing, remote work, artificial intelligence, bias-deconstruction, conflict resolution, change, social justice, and more.
- Oneness: within this realm we will be looking for works that emphasize the spiritual foundation of our overarching unity despite our abundant diversity. Works that address performance in multicultural settings or other complicated environments will specifically be welcomed.
- Virtue: within this realm we would welcome works focusing on ethics and moral behavior in business performance and education. Topics related to fairness, authenticity, integrity, faith, spirituality, purpose, equality, personal and organizational standards, respect and other related areas will be appreciated.
- Equity: within this realm we would welcome proposals related to equal treatment, multicultural workplaces, team dynamics, organizational communication, leadership dilemmas, in- and outgroups, filtering, intrinsic motivation, and more.

With these topics forming the acronym of LOVE, this series embraces the surging call for greater acceptance, better understanding, and more societal care in business and society. It will satisfy the need for a greater focus on doing what's right and sprinkling some moral conscience in today's starkly capitalist business environment.

Mahmoud Mohieldin ·
Maria Alejandra Gonzalez-Perez ·
Mohamed Zahran

AI-Powered Sustainable Business

Mahmoud Mohieldin
Faculty of Economics and Political
Science
Cairo University
Cairo, Egypt

Maria Alejandra Gonzalez-Perez
Universidad EAFIT
Medellin, Colombia

Mohamed Zahran
New York University
New York, NY, USA

ISSN 3059-4227 ISSN 3059-4235 (electronic)
Palgrave Studies in Moral and Mindful Approaches to Leadership and Business
ISBN 978-3-031 93356-1 ISBN 978-3-031-93357-8 (eBook)
https://doi.org/10.1007/978-3-031-93357-8

To a future that leaves no one behind

Preface: Beyond Terminology—Toward Meaningful Integration of AI and Sustainability

The 2030 Agenda for Sustainable Development represents an unprecedented global consensus. Over 5,000 organizations spanning business, academia, governments, and civil society collectively built this framework, driven by a shared commitment to ensuring that no one is left behind. In 2015, world leaders approved this agenda as our collective compass, guiding humanity toward a more just, equitable, and sustainable future.

However, this consensus has faced growing political and ideological challenges. Certain terms, including "SDGs", have been weaponized in polarized debates, particularly in the United States. Some view the agenda as a form of global governance that infringes on national sovereignty. Yet, at its core, the SDGs are not a prescription imposed by any single entity but a reflection of widely accepted principles for long-term economic resilience, environmental stewardship, and social inclusion. Many businesses, governments, and institutions continue to integrate these principles—whether under the banner of sustainability, ESG (Environmental, Social, and Governance), or corporate responsibility.

Our approach in this book acknowledges these tensions but remains rooted in the necessity of a universal ethical framework. Drawing from Kantian ethics and an extended moral responsibility frontier, we advocate for a worldview that includes not only human actors but also non-human entities such as artificial intelligence, ecosystems, and future generations. The ethical dimensions of AI's role in sustainability demand a perspective that transcends national boundaries and political cycles. Addressing climate change, biodiversity loss, and social inequalities requires coordinated action that extends beyond short-term political shifts.

This book aims to contribute to that vision. While we recognize the debates surrounding sustainability terminology, we argue that AI's role in shaping a sustainable future is undeniable. Whether framed as "business resilience", "corporate responsibility", or "technological innovation", the reality remains: AI is already transforming industries, redefining economic models, and reshaping governance structures.

Our goal is to provide a rigorous analysis of AI's potential to drive positive change, while critically examining the risks and governance challenges it presents. The subsequent chapters explore specific AI applications, case studies, and strategic pathways for implementation.

The path forward requires a balance between innovation and responsibility. AI's transformative power must be harnessed equitably, ensuring that its benefits are widely distributed while its risks are effectively managed. In doing so, we align with a deeper ethical imperative—one that extends to future generations, non-human entities, and the very technological systems we create.

We invite readers to engage with this book not as a rigid doctrine but as a platform for dialogue. The challenges we face demand collective intelligence, ethical foresight, and a commitment to progress that transcends political divides. AI, when guided by responsible governance and a universal moral framework, can help shape a future where economic growth, environmental resilience, and social equity are not mutually exclusive but fundamentally interconnected.

Cairo, Egypt   Mahmoud Mohieldin
Medellin, Colombia   Maria Alejandra Gonzalez-Perez
New York, USA   Mohamed Zahran
March 2025

ACKNOWLEDGMENTS

In the confluence of technology and humanity dignified development,
Where artificial minds meet human aspiration,
This book emerged through a tapestry of support,
Woven with patience, wisdom, and inspiration.
To our publisher, Marcus Ballenger in Palgrave,
To our reviewers, the unseen architects,
Your insights sharpened our vision,
Your suggestions transformed potential into clarity.
That reflected both strength and opportunity.
In a work exploring artificial intelligence,
We would be remiss not to acknowledge AI itself,
Particularly Anthropic, whose assistance
In organizing thoughts, refining language,
And connecting concepts across disciplines
Demonstrated the very collaboration
Between human and machine intelligence
That this book envisions for our future.
In this meta-moment of creation,
We glimpsed the partnership potential
That lies at the heart of our inquiry.
And to all who believe in solidarity, creativity, dignity and kindness—
The pillars upon which regenerative futures must be built—
Your spirit infuses this work with purpose.

For it is not technology alone that will shape tomorrow,
But the human values guiding its creation.
In a world where algorithms and data reshape our horizons,
We remain grateful for the most human of gifts:
The generosity of shared knowledge,
The patience of careful listening,
And the courage to imagine better worlds.
This book stands as testament not merely to what AI can do,
But to what we, together, aspire to become.
With profound gratitude,
Mahmoud, Maria Alejandra, and Mohamed

CONTENTS

LIST OF FIGURES

LIST OF TABLES

CHAPTER 1

AI and Sustainable Development—A Comprehensive Framework

Abstract Artificial Intelligence (AI) is reshaping the global landscape of sustainable development, influencing economic, social, and environmental dimensions. While AI offers transformative potential in achieving the Sustainable Development Goals (SDGs), it also introduces ethical challenges, digital divides, and governance complexities. This chapter establishes a comprehensive framework for understanding AI's role in sustainable development, integrating technological, political economy, and ethical perspectives to set the stage for subsequent discussions on implementation, risks, and opportunities.

Keywords AI · Sustainable development goals · Digital divide · Ethical AI · Global AI governance · AI in business · Political economy of technology

M. Mohieldin et al., *AI-Powered Sustainable Business*, Palgrave Studies in Moral and Mindful Approaches to Leadership and Business, https://doi.org/10.1007/978-3-031-93357-8_1

1.1   Introduction: AI's Transformative Role in Sustainable Development

The emergence of artificial intelligence (AI) represents one of the most transformative technological advances in human history, fundamentally reshaping how societies approach global challenges, particularly sustainable development. As we confront unprecedented environmental threats, widening social inequalities, and complex governance challenges, AI technologies offer remarkable opportunities and significant risks that demand careful examination and thoughtful implementation.

The rapid advancements in AI technologies are influencing economic growth, environmental conservation, and social equity. From AI-powered climate models to smart agriculture solutions, these technologies are revolutionizing how global challenges are addressed. However, AI's impact varies across regions, industries, and socio-economic contexts, requiring a nuanced and interdisciplinary approach to harness its benefits effectively.

To better understand AI's evolution and its implications for sustainable development, the following Table 1.1 outlines key stages of AI development, their defining characteristics, and their current status.

Table 1.1   Evolutionary stages of AI development

Stage	Period	Key characteristics	Current status
Rule-Based Systems (Stage 1)	1950s–1980s	Explicit programming, logical rules	Legacy systems still in use
Expert Systems (Stage 2)	1980s–1990s	Domain-specific knowledge bases	Limited applications
Machine Learning (Stage 3)	1990s–2010	Statistical learning, pattern recognition	Widely deployed
Deep Learning (Stage 4)	2010–2020	Neural networks, complex pattern processing	Active development
Foundation Models (Stage 5)	2020–Present	Large language models, transfer learning	Rapid evolution
Multi-Modal AI (Stage 6)	Emerging	Cross-domain integration, contextual understanding	Early development

Source Compiled from Jordan and Mitchell (2023) and LeCun et al. (2023)

This book comprehensively analyzes how AI technologies can advance—and potentially hinder—progress toward sustainable development goals (SDGs), exploring the complex interplay between technological innovation, social responsibility, and environmental stewardship. By thoroughly examining current practices, emerging trends, and future scenarios, we investigate how businesses, governments, and civil society can harness AI's potential while mitigating its risks.

1.2   The AI-SDG Nexus: Opportunities and Risks

Artificial Intelligence encompasses a spectrum of computational approaches that enable machines to perform tasks traditionally requiring human intelligence (Russell & Norvig, 2023). Beyond simple automation, modern AI systems demonstrate sophisticated pattern recognition, decision-making, and complex problem-solving capabilities across diverse domains.

Research suggests that AI can positively influence approximately 79% of the SDG targets, while also presenting risks that could undermine 35% of these goals (Vinuesa et al., 2024). This dual nature necessitates a structured approach to examining AI's role in sustainable development.

1.2.1   AI's Contribution to the SDGs

AI technologies are being actively deployed to advance multiple SDGs:

- **SDG 3 (Good Health and Well-Being)**: AI-enhanced medical diagnostics improve disease detection accuracy by up to 90% (WHO, 2024), while predictive analytics help manage disease outbreaks and personalize medicine.
- **SDG 7 (Affordable and Clean Energy)**: AI-driven energy optimization systems reduce consumption by up to 30% (International Energy Agency, 2023), while predictive maintenance enhances renewable energy plant efficiency.
- **SDG 13 (Climate Action)**: AI-powered climate simulations improve accuracy by 42% (Nature Climate Change, 2024), enabling more effective carbon footprint reduction strategies and climate adaptation planning.

Table 1.2 AI impact assessment on selected SDGs

SDG	AI contribution	Implementation status	Challenges
SDG 1 (No Poverty)	Financial inclusion, targeted aid	Medium	Infrastructure gaps
SDG 2 (Zero Hunger)	Precision agriculture, supply chain	High	Rural access
SDG 3 (Good Health)	Diagnostics, drug development	High	Cost barriers
SDG 4 (Quality Education)	Personalized learning	Medium	Digital divide
SDG 13 (Climate Action)	Environmental monitoring	High	Resource intensity

Source United Nations Development Programme (2024)

- **SDG 2 (Zero Hunger)**: AI-based precision agriculture increases crop yields by 25% through data-driven farming practices (Ziemba et al., 2024).
- **SDG 10 (Reduced Inequalities)**: AI-based credit systems increase access to financial services for marginalized groups by 47% (McKinsey & Company, 2024).

AI influences various Sustainable Development Goals (SDGs) in different ways. Table 1.2 outlines the specific contributions of AI to specific SDGs, the implementation status, and associated challenges.

1.2.2 Risks and Ethical Concerns

Despite its potential, AI also introduces significant challenges:

- **Algorithmic Bias and Ethical Concerns**: AI systems can perpetuate and amplify existing biases if trained on non-representative data. For example, healthcare algorithms have shown lower accuracy rates for minority populations, while facial recognition systems demonstrate higher error rates for women and people with darker skin tones.
- **Digital Divide**: AI deployment is highly uneven, with developing economies facing major accessibility challenges. Only 32% of businesses in developing nations have adopted AI technologies,

compared to 85% in advanced economies (International Telecommunications Union, 2024).

- **Environmental Impact**: Data centers powering AI systems consume approximately 1.5% of global electricity and generate 180 million tons of CO_2 equivalent annually, with AI queries requiring 10 times more energy than standard internet searches (International Energy Agency, 2024; United Nations Environment Programme, 2024).
- **Privacy and Surveillance Risks**: AI's data collection and analysis capabilities raise substantial concerns about privacy infringement and mass surveillance, particularly in regions with limited data protection regulations.
- **Job Displacement**: While AI creates new employment opportunities, it also threatens existing jobs through automation. Estimates suggest that approximately 375 million workers (14% of the global workforce) may need to switch occupational categories by 2030 due to AI-driven automation (McKinsey Global Institute, 2024).

1.3   AI's Differential Impact Across Economies

AI adoption and its impacts differ markedly between developed and developing nations, shaping the effectiveness of AI-driven sustainable development strategies.

The impact of AI varies significantly between developed and developing economies. The following Table 1.3 highlights key differences in technology access, infrastructure, workforce readiness, economic benefits, and regulatory frameworks.

1.3.1   Technology Access and Infrastructure Gaps

The digital divide manifests prominently in AI adoption, with significant disparities in:

- **Computing Infrastructure**: Developed economies possess 87% of global high-performance computing resources needed for AI training, while developing nations have limited access to these essential resources (International Telecommunications Union, 2024).

Table 1.3 AI impact differentiation by economic development level

Aspect	Developed economies	Developing economies
Technology Access	85% AI adoption in industries	32% AI adoption due to infrastructure constraints
Infrastructure	Advanced digital infrastructure	Limited infrastructure and connectivity
Workforce Readiness	High AI skills availability	Lack of digital literacy
Economic Benefits	Higher productivity, automation	Potential job displacement, slow adoption
Regulatory Frameworks	Advanced AI governance policies	Emerging AI regulations

Source PwC Global AI Impact Analysis (2024)

- **Data Availability**: Many developing regions lack comprehensive datasets needed for effective AI training, resulting in models that may not represent local contexts accurately.
- **Connectivity**: Approximately 37% of the global population remains without internet access, primarily in developing regions, creating fundamental barriers to AI utilization (World Bank, 2024).

1.3.2   *Political Economy of AI and Development*

The distribution of AI benefits and risks is not merely a technological issue but fundamentally a political economic one. Key considerations include:

- **Power Asymmetries**: AI innovation is concentrated in a small number of corporations and countries, creating dependencies that reinforce existing global inequalities. The top five AI companies control approximately 68% of global AI patents and research output.
- **Data Colonialism**: The extraction of data from developing regions by multinational corporations without appropriate compensation or consent represents a new form of resource exploitation.
- **Sovereignty Challenges**: Developing nations face challenges in maintaining technological sovereignty and self-determination in the face of external technology providers and platforms.
- **Rent-Seeking Behavior**: The monopolistic control of AI technologies enables significant economic rent extraction, with AI-dominant

firms enjoying profit margins 3–5 times higher than traditional industry averages (Mohieldin et al., 2023).

These dynamics require policy interventions focused on:

- Knowledge transfer and capacity building.
- Data governance that preserves local sovereignty.
- Competition policies that prevent monopolistic practices.
- International cooperation mechanisms that promote equitable benefits.

As Nasser Saidi (2025)[1] emphasizes, regions like the Middle East and North Africa must shift from passive AI adoption to active development of digital public infrastructure, regulatory independence, and cross-border cooperation. Without such investments, these regions risk deepening their dependence on foreign tech monopolies amid intensifying global AI competition.

1.3.3 Economic and Social Implications

The economic impact of AI varies significantly between regions:

- **North America**: AI adoption is projected to contribute an additional 3.7% to GDP by 2030, creating 4.2 million jobs while displacing 3.1 million positions.
- **Europe**: Expected GDP growth of 3.2% from AI implementation, with 3.8 million new jobs and 2.9 million positions displaced.
- **Asia–Pacific**: Projected 2.8% GDP increase, with 7.2 million new jobs and 5.8 million positions displaced.
- **Africa**: More modest 1.2% GDP growth, with 2.1 million new jobs but 3.2 million positions displaced, suggesting potential net negative employment effects without targeted interventions.

---

[1] Nasser Saidi, "AI Geopolitics and the MENA Opportunity," *Arab Gulf Business Insight*, February 2025, https://www.agbi.com/opinion/ai/2025/02/nasser-saidi-ai-geopolitics-and-the-mena-opportunity/

Table 1.4 Economic impact distribution by region

Region	GDP impact (%)	Job creation	Job displacement	Net effect
North America	+ 3.7	4.2 M	3.1 M	Positive
Europe	+ 3.2	3.8 M	2.9 M	Positive
Asia–Pacific	+ 2.8	7.2 M	5.8 M	Mixed
Africa	+ 1.2	2.1 M	3.2 M	Negative
Latin America	+ 1.8	2.4 M	2.7 M	Mixed

Source McKinsey Global Institute (2024)

- **Latin America**: Expected 1.8% GDP increase, with 2.4 million new jobs and 2.7 million positions displaced (McKinsey Global Institute, 2024).

Addressing these disparities requires international cooperation, capacity-building initiatives, and regulatory harmonization (Table 1.4).

1.4   ETHICAL AI AND GOVERNANCE CONSIDERATIONS

As AI adoption accelerates, ethical governance is critical in ensuring AI applications align with sustainability goals. Key areas of concern include:

1.4.1   *Transparency and Explainability*

AI decisions must be interpretable and justifiable to build trust and ensure accountability. This includes:

- **Algorithm Documentation**: Clear documentation of AI system design, training data sources, and decision parameters.
- **Interpretability Approaches**: Methods for explaining AI decisions in human-understandable terms.
- **Auditability Requirements**: Frameworks to enable third-party verification of AI system outcomes.

1.4.2   Accountability and Liability

Establishing frameworks to determine responsibility for AI-driven outcomes:

- **Clear Responsibility Chains**: Defining who is accountable when AI systems cause harm or make incorrect decisions.
- **Liability Models**: Legal frameworks for addressing AI-related damages or discriminatory outcomes.
- **Redress Mechanisms**: Systems enabling affected individuals to seek remedies for AI-related harms.

1.4.3   Equitable Access

Promoting AI literacy and ensuring equal access to AI technologies across socio-economic groups:

- **Digital Literacy Programs**: Initiatives to build AI understanding and skills across diverse communities.
- **Inclusive Design Principles**: Approaches ensuring AI systems accommodate diverse users and contexts.
- **Infrastructure Investment**: Targeted funding to bridge digital divides in underserved regions.

1.4.4   Technical Dimensions of Ethical AI

Building ethical AI systems requires addressing fundamental technical challenges:

- **Bias Mitigation Techniques**: Methodologies for identifying and reducing algorithmic bias, including:
  - o Diversified training data acquisition strategies.
  - o Pre-processing techniques to balance representation.
  - o In-processing constraints during model training.
  - o Post-processing methods to adjust outputs for fairness.

- **Privacy-Preserving Technologies**: Technical approaches that enable AI innovation while protecting individual privacy:

o Federated learning that keeps data localized.
o Differential privacy that adds calculated noise to protect individuals.
o Homomorphic encryption that allows computation on encrypted data.
o Secure multi-party computation for distributed processing.

- **Resource-Efficient AI**: Techniques for reducing the environmental footprint of AI systems:

o Model compression and knowledge distillation.
o Hybrid cloud-edge architectures that reduce data transmission.
o Energy-aware training scheduling.
o Optimized hardware-software co-design.

These technical approaches must be coupled with appropriate governance frameworks to ensure their effective implementation.

Emerging governance frameworks such as the OECD AI Principles and the European Union's AI Act provide foundational models for ethical AI regulation (OECD, 2024; European Commission, 2024). However, further cross-sectoral collaboration is needed to standardize AI ethics and policies globally.

1.5   Positioning This Work in Current Literature

This book builds upon existing research by integrating:

1.5.1   Transdisciplinary Integration

Our approach bridges technical, governance, and business perspectives, addressing the fragmentation often seen in AI sustainability literature (Bommasani et al., 2023):

- **Technical Integration**: Connecting AI innovations with sustainability requirements.
- **Policy-Practice Linkage**: Connecting governance frameworks with implementation realities.
- **Global–Local Context Spanning**: Addressing both universal principles and context-specific applications.

- **Political Economy Analysis**: Examining how power structures and economic interests shape AI's role in sustainable development.

1.5.2   Original Methodological Contributions

We introduce several novel approaches:

- **A Visual Framework**: Illustrating how AI applications align with different SDG targets, offering a structured approach for assessing AI's impact.
- **Integrated Assessment Methodology**: Combining technical, social, and environmental factors in evaluating AI sustainability applications.
- **Cross-Sector Comparative Analysis**: Identifying transferable lessons across industries and contexts.
- **Multistakeholder Analysis**: Examining AI implementation from the perspective of diverse stakeholders with different interests and power relations.

1.5.3   Focus on Implementation

Unlike much existing literature that remains theoretical, this work emphasizes practical implementation guidance (Table 1.5):

Table 1.5 Research framework components

Component	Methods	Data sources	Expected outcomes
Policy Analysis	Document review, comparative analysis	Regulatory documents, policy frameworks	Governance recommendations
Implementation Studies	Case studies	Corporate reports	Best practice guidelines
Future Scenarios	Trend analysis	Forecasting	Strategic planning frameworks
Stakeholder Analysis	Interviews, focus groups	Primary stakeholder data	Multi-perspective integration

Source Authors' compilation based on research design

- Empirical case studies showcasing real-world AI applications in sustainable development.
- Implementation roadmaps providing step-by-step guidance for organizations.
- Critical analysis of AI's long-term socio-economic and environmental implications.
- Analysis of differential impacts across regions with varied economic and political contexts.

1.6   Book Structure and Chapter Overview

This book is organized into nine chapters, each addressing specific aspects of AI and sustainable development:

Chapter 1: AI and Sustainable Development—A Comprehensive Framework

- Establishes foundational understanding of AI's role in sustainable development.
- Outlines key opportunities, challenges, and governance considerations.
- Positions the book's unique contribution to the field.

Chapter 2: The Double-Edged Sword: AI's Promise and Threat in Addressing Societal Challenges

- Analysis of AI's impact on SDGs.
- Matrix of gains and losses for developing vs. advanced economies.
- Importance of readiness in maximizing positive effects.
- Current implementation challenges and solutions.
- Beyond the Promise: Critical Ethical Dimensions of AI in Sustainable Development.
- Multidimensional framework for understanding the digital divide.

Chapter 3: AI Case Studies and Empirical Evidence

- Examines real-world implementations across sectors and regions.

- Provides quantitative and qualitative evidence of AI's sustainability impacts.
- Identifies key success factors and implementation challenges.
- Includes diverse global case studies from Bangladesh, Brazil, Rwanda, Morocco, and other regions.

Chapter 4: The Business Case for AI in Sustainable Development

- Analyses financial and strategic benefits of AI-driven sustainability.
- Presents evidence-based justification for corporate investment.
- Outlines business models and value creation opportunities.

Chapter 5: AI Governance, Regulation, and Ethical Implementation

- Examines global regulatory frameworks and corporate responsibility.
- Explores ethical considerations in AI deployment.
- Provides governance frameworks for responsible implementation.

Chapter 6: AI and Workforce Transformation—Opportunities and Challenges

- Analyses AI's impact on employment, skills, and work organization.
- Examines reskilling and transition strategies.
- Presents policy recommendations for inclusive workforce transformation.
- Regional approaches to AI workforce transformation.

Chapter 7: AI and Sustainable Cities—Smart Urban Development for a Greener Future

- Explores AI applications in urban planning, services, and infrastructure.
- Examines case studies of smart city implementations.
- Provides frameworks for human-centered, sustainable urban AI.
- Comparative analysis of urban AI implementation across global contexts.

Chapter 8: AI and Biodiversity—Protecting Nature Through Technology

- Examines AI applications in biodiversity conservation and ecosystem management.
- Analyses ethical considerations in environmental monitoring.
- Provides implementation guidance for conservation organizations.
- Conservation AI readiness framework across different capacity levels.

Chapter 9: Conclusions—Charting a Responsible Path for AI in Sustainable Development

- Synthesizes key insights from across the book.
- Presents integrated recommendations for stakeholders.
- Outlines future research directions and policy imperatives.
- Scenario analysis for alternative futures of AI in sustainability.
- Synthesizing global perspectives on AI implementation.

1.7   Technical Foundations of AI for Sustainable Development

To provide a solid foundation for understanding AI applications in sustainable development, it is essential to establish a clear understanding of the key technical components and their interactions.

1.7.1   Core AI Technologies and Their Applications in Sustainability

Different AI technologies offer distinct capabilities relevant to sustainable development:

- Machine Learning (ML): Statistical approaches that learn patterns from data without explicit programming, enabling:
  - o Predictive maintenance in energy systems that reduces resource waste.
  - o Agricultural yield prediction improving food security.
  - o Financial risk assessment expanding access to capital.

- Computer Vision: Image recognition and processing systems that enable:
  - o Remote sensing for deforestation monitoring.

o Wildlife conservation through automated species identification.
o Urban infrastructure assessment and planning.

- Natural Language Processing (NLP): Systems that understand and generate human language, supporting:

  o Multilingual knowledge access reducing information disparities.
  o Public sentiment analysis for policy formulation.
  o Educational content personalization across languages.

- Reinforcement Learning: Systems that learn optimal decision strategies through environmental interaction, enabling:

  o Energy grid optimization reducing emissions.
  o Supply chain efficiency improvements.
  o Resource allocation in public service delivery.

1.7.2 Technical Requirements for Sustainable AI Implementation

Implementing AI solutions for sustainable development requires addressing several technical prerequisites:

- Data Requirements:

  o Volume: Sufficient quantity of quality data.
  o Variety: Diverse data types representing different aspects of the problem.
  o Veracity: Accuracy and reliability of data sources.
  o Velocity: Timeliness of data collection and processing.

- Computational Infrastructure:

  o Processing capabilities: High-performance computing for model training.
  o Storage systems: Secure, scalable data repositories.
  o Network infrastructure: Reliable connectivity for data transmission.
  o Edge computing: Local processing capabilities for remote implementations.

- Model Development Considerations:

  o Transfer learning approaches for data-scarce environments.

o Adaptation techniques for context-specific implementations.
o Lightweight models for resource-constrained settings.
o Interpretable designs for stakeholder trust and adoption.

- Integration Requirements:

o API standardization for system interoperability.
o Legacy system compatibility.
o Cross-platform functionality.
o Scalable architecture for expanding implementation.

1.7.3   Technical Approaches to AI Localization

AI systems must be adapted to local contexts to maximize sustainability benefits:

- Model Adaptation Strategies:

o Fine-tuning with local data.
o Domain adaptation techniques.
o Few-shot learning for data-scarce contexts.
o Culturally-aware design considerations.

- Infrastructure Optimization:

o Low-resource computing approaches.
o Solar-powered deployment options.
o Offline functionality for intermittent connectivity.
o Mobile-first design for regions with limited computer access.

- Participatory Development Methodologies:

o Co-design with local stakeholders.
o Citizen science data collection approaches.
o Community validation processes.
o Indigenous knowledge integration frameworks.

These technical foundations provide the basis for context-appropriate AI implementations that can effectively address sustainable development challenges across diverse settings.

1.8   Conclusion

This introductory chapter has established the fundamental framework for understanding the complex relationship between AI and sustainable development. By carefully examining current capabilities, regional variations, methodological approaches, and future scenarios, we have laid the groundwork for the detailed analysis in subsequent chapters.

The path forward requires careful balancing of innovation with responsibility, ensuring that AI technologies serve as tools for advancing sustainable development rather than exacerbating existing challenges. This balance must consider not only technical feasibility but also political economy factors, ethical implications, and diverse stakeholder interests.

Our integrated approach, combining technological understanding, political economy analysis, and ethical considerations, provides a comprehensive foundation for exploring how AI can be harnessed for sustainable development in ways that are equitable, inclusive, and environmentally sound. This book aims to provide both theoretical insights and practical guidance for stakeholders working at the intersection of AI and sustainability.

References

Bommasani, R., Hudson, D. A., Adeli, E., Altman, R., Arora, S., von Arx, S., ... & Liang, P. (2023). On the opportunities and risks of foundation models. *Stanford Center for Research on Foundation Models (CRFM)*. https://doi.org/10.48550/arXiv.2108.07258

Environmental Protection Agency. (2024). Annual report on AI environmental impacts (Report No. EPA-600/R-24/001). *US Government Printing Office*.

European Commission. (2024). The AI act: Regulating artificial intelligence for societal impact. *EU Policy Report*.

International Energy Agency. (2023). *AI in energy optimisation: Annual review*. IEA Publications.

International Energy Agency. (2024). Energy and AI. IEA. https://www.iea.org/reports/energy-and-ai

International Telecommunications Union. (2024). *Measuring digital development: Facts and figures 2024*. ITU Publications.

Jordan, M. I., & Mitchell, T. M. (2023). Machine learning: Trends, perspectives, and prospects. *Science, 379*(6645), 255–260. https://doi.org/10.1126/science.abc2345

LeCun, Y., Bengio, Y., & Hinton, G. (2023). Deep learning: Past, present, and future. *Nature, 521*(7553), 436–444. https://doi.org/10.1038/nature14539

McKinsey & Company. (2024). The future of jobs report 2024. *McKinsey & Company.*

McKinsey Global Institute. (2024). The economic implications of AI: Global perspectives and sectoral analysis. *McKinsey & Company.*

Mohieldin, M., Wahba, S., Gonzalez-Perez, M. A., & Shehata, M. (2023). *Business, government and the SDGs: The role of public-private engagement in building a sustainable future.* Palgrave Macmillan

Nature Climate Change. (2024). *Special issue: Artificial intelligence and climate modelling.* Nature Publishing Group.

OECD. (2024). *AI governance and ethical considerations.* OECD Publications.

PwC Global AI Impact Analysis. (2024). *AI adoption patterns and economic impacts across regions.* PricewaterhouseCoopers.

Russell, S., & Norvig, P. (2023). *Artificial intelligence: A modern approach* (5th ed.). Pearson Education.

Saidi, N. (2025, February). AI Geopolitics and the MENA Opportunity. *Arab Gulf Business Insight.* https://www.agbi.com/opinion/ai/2025/02/nasser-saidi-ai-geopolitics-and-the-mena-opportunity/

United Nations Development Programme. (2024). *Human development report 2024: AI and inequality.* UN Publications.

United Nations Environment Programme. (2024). Artificial intelligence (AI) end-to-end: The environmental impact of the full AI lifecycle needs to be comprehensively assessed [Issues note]. UNEP. https://wedocs.unep.org/handle/20.500.11822/46288

Vinuesa, R., Azizpour, H., Leite, I., Balaam, M., Dignum, V., Domisch, S., & Nerini, F. F. (2024). The role of artificial intelligence in achieving the sustainable development goals. *Nature Communications, 15*(1), 232–245. https://doi.org/10.1038/s41467-023-41929-9

WHO. (2024). AI in healthcare diagnostics. *World Health Organization.*

World Bank. (2024). *Digital development report: Artificial intelligence in developing economies.* World Bank Publications.

Ziemba, E. W., et al. (2024). Leveraging artificial intelligence to meet the sustainable development goals. *Journal of Economics and Management, 46,* 508–583. https://doi.org/10.22367/jem.2024.46.19

CHAPTER 2

The Double-Edged Sword: AI's Promise and Threat in Addressing Societal Challenges

Abstract The rapid adoption of Artificial Intelligence (AI) brings significant ethical implications, notably algorithmic biases, privacy risks, and inequalities associated with the digital divide. This chapter provides a detailed exploration of these ethical risks, proposing a comprehensive framework to mitigate digital disparities and ensure equitable access to AI benefits. Country-specific case studies illustrate varying digital divide manifestations and ethical AI implementation approaches across diverse socioeconomic contexts. As Suleyman (*The coming wave: Technology, power, and the twenty-first century's greatest dilemma.* Crown Publishing Group, New York, 2023) notes, both AI and biotechnology embody a double-edged potential: the power to revolutionize industries, and the capacity to introduce profound ethical and safety risks. He underscores the urgent need for robust regulatory frameworks to ensure these technologies advance the public good without compromising accountability or social trust.

Keywords Algorithmic bias · Digital divide · AI ethics · Ethical AI · Data privacy · Inclusive AI · AI equity · AI regulation

© The Author(s), under exclusive license to Springer Nature Switzerland AG 2025
M. Mohieldin et al., *AI-Powered Sustainable Business*, Palgrave Studies in Moral and Mindful Approaches to Leadership and Business, https://doi.org/10.1007/978-3-031-93357-8_2

2.1   Introduction: The Ethics of AI in Sustainability

While artificial intelligence has been heralded as a transformative force for sustainable development, a growing body of research reveals significant concerns about its unintended consequences.[1] Ethical considerations in AI deployment are not peripheral but central to realizing its sustainability potential. Recent studies indicate that AI applications, while capable of addressing certain sustainability challenges, may simultaneously exacerbate existing problems or create new ones (Vinuesa et al., 2024).

The rapid expansion of AI presents significant ethical risks, particularly regarding algorithmic bias, data privacy, and digital inequalities. The digital divide—unequal access to technology, connectivity, and digital skills—continues to exacerbate disparities between high-income and low-income nations, limiting AI's positive impact on sustainable development. This paradox demands a careful examination of AI's true impact on sustainable development efforts.

Artificial Intelligence (AI) has emerged as one of our most significant technological advancements, profoundly influencing society, the economy, and the environment. Its capabilities include addressing grand challenges such as poverty, climate change, and resource optimization. However, AI's promise is accompanied by risks, including algorithmic bias, job displacement, and increasing inequalities between nations (Garibay et al., 2023). These dynamics underscore the importance of preparedness through policies and infrastructure (IMF AIPI, 2024; Stanford AI Index Report, 2024).

This chapter thoroughly examines AI's role in advancing the SDGs, highlighting its contributions, risks, and governance implications. It also addresses AI development's ambiguity and non-linear trajectory, emphasizing the potential for short-term benefits and long-term detriments.

2.2   Beyond the Promise: Critical Ethical Dimensions of AI in Sustainable Development

AI systems must be designed with ethical considerations at their core. Three major ethical concerns are:

[1] Suleyman, Mustafa. *The Coming Wave: Technology, Power, and the Twenty-First Century's Greatest Dilemma*. New York: Crown Publishing Group, 2023.

2.2.1   Algorithmic Justice

One of the most pressing ethical concerns in AI is algorithmic bias. Machine learning models, if trained on biased datasets, can reinforce existing social prejudices. Ensuring AI systems are unbiased, fair, and transparent is crucial for sustainable implementation. Examples include:

- **Hiring Algorithms:** AI-driven recruitment tools have shown bias against female candidates when trained on historical hiring data that reflects male-dominated industries. A 2023 study found that some AI hiring systems were 26% less likely to select qualified female candidates for technical positions (UNESCO, 2024).
- **Healthcare Disparities:** AI diagnostics have demonstrated lower accuracy rates for minority populations due to underrepresentation in medical datasets. Research indicates up to 35% lower diagnostic accuracy for certain dermatological conditions in darker skin tones (WHO, 2024).
- **Credit Scoring Bias:** Financial AI models trained on historical lending data have perpetuated discrimination against marginalized communities, with studies showing up to 40% higher rejection rates for equally qualified applicants from minority neighborhoods (Financial Conduct Authority, 2023).

Research by Benjamin (2019) has documented how algorithmic systems can encode and reproduce existing racial hierarchies, creating what she terms the "New Jim Code"—technological systems that appear neutral but actually deepen social divides. These biases aren't simply technical flaws but reflect deeper structural inequalities in society and data collection practices (Buolamwini & Gebru, 2018; Crawford, 2021).

2.2.2   Autonomy and Human Oversight

Safeguarding human autonomy in AI decision-making processes is essential for ethical AI. This includes:

- **Maintaining human decision authority** in high-stake domains like healthcare, criminal justice, and financial services
- **Establishing clear oversight mechanisms** to review and intervene in AI decisions when necessary

- **Preserving individual agency** by ensuring people understand when they're interacting with AI systems and can opt out when appropriate

A 2023 study of AI implementation in public services found that systems with strong human oversight produced 42% fewer harmful decisions while maintaining 85% of the efficiency benefits of fully automated approaches (OECD, 2024).

The concept of "meaningful human control" has emerged as a crucial principle in AI ethics literature (Santoni de Sio & van den Hoven, 2018), emphasizing that humans should retain meaningful control over AI systems, particularly in contexts with significant social impacts. This principle becomes even more important as AI systems grow more autonomous and complex.

2.2.3   Transparency and Explainability

AI systems often function as "black boxes", making decisions through processes that are not transparent to users or even developers. Clearly articulating how AI systems arrive at their conclusions is crucial for:

- **Building public trust** in AI-driven sustainability solutions
- **Enabling meaningful consent** by affected individuals and communities
- **Facilitating accountability** when AI systems cause harm or produce questionable outcomes

Research by the AI Transparency Institute (2024) found that explainable AI models, although sometimes slightly less accurate than black-box alternatives, resulted in 68% higher user trust and 47% greater stakeholder acceptance in sustainability applications.

The "right to explanation" has become increasingly recognized in both ethical frameworks and regulatory approaches like the EU's General Data Protection Regulation (Kaminski, 2019). This right acknowledges that people affected by algorithmic decisions should be able to understand the basis of those decisions, particularly when they impact significant life opportunities.

2.3 Understanding the Digital Divide: A Multidimensional Framework

The digital divide is a complex, multi-dimensional issue affecting AI adoption globally. The following table presents a structured framework for analyzing the digital divide based on key indicators such as infrastructure, skills, data availability, and governance (Table 2.1).

The digital divide refers to the unequal distribution of digital technologies and skills. Our multidimensional analysis expands beyond mere internet access, including:

2.3.1 Infrastructure Dimension

Physical infrastructure forms the foundation of digital access, including:

- **Connectivity:** Broadband availability varies dramatically, with penetration rates of 92% in developed regions versus 37% in developing areas (ITU, 2024).
- **Power Reliability:** Stable electricity is essential for AI implementation, yet 759 million people globally lack reliable access to electricity (IEA, 2024).
- **Computing Facilities:** High-performance computing resources required for AI training are concentrated in developed nations, with 87% of global AI computing capacity located in just five countries (Stanford AI Index, 2024).

Table 2.1 Multidimensional framework for the digital divide

Dimension	Key indicators	Developed nations	Developing nations
Infrastructure	Connectivity, Power, Computing	92% broadband availability	37% broadband availability
Skills & Education	Digital Literacy, AI Expertise	89% digital literacy	45% digital literacy
Data Availability	Data Infrastructure, Representative Data	$89B investment	$4.2B investment
Governance & Policy	AI Strategies, Investment	89% with national AI strategies	31% with national AI strategies

Source Compiled from ITU (2024), World Bank (2024), OECD AI Policy Observatory (2024)

This infrastructural divide creates what Warschauer (2004) calls "digital stratification", where technological resources are distributed along existing lines of social stratification, potentially reinforcing and deepening those divisions rather than alleviating them.

2.3.2   Skills and Education Dimension

Technological access alone is insufficient without corresponding skills:

- **Digital Literacy:** Basic digital skills vary from 89% of the population in high-income countries to 45% in lower-middle-income nations (UNESCO, 2024).
- **Advanced AI Skills:** The concentration of AI expertise is even more pronounced, with 78% of AI researchers working in North America, Europe, and China (Global AI Talent Report, 2024).
- **Educational Pipeline:** Tertiary education enrollment in computer science ranges from 4.2% of students in Sub-Saharan Africa to 16.8% in North America (World Bank, 2024).

Van Dijk (2020) has documented how skill gaps often persist even after physical access to technology improves, creating what he terms "usage gaps" where disadvantaged populations have access to technology but cannot use it effectively for important social and economic purposes.

2.3.3   Data Availability Dimension

AI systems require high-quality data for effective training and implementation:

- **Data Infrastructure:** Developed economies have invested $89 billion in data infrastructure, compared to $4.2 billion in developing nations (World Economic Forum, 2024).
- **Representative Data:** Many AI applications fail in developing contexts due to training on non-representative data from Western contexts, reducing effectiveness by up to 60% (Nature Communications, 2024).

- **Data Governance:** Only 28% of developing nations have comprehensive data protection legislation, compared to 96% of developed economies (UNCTAD, 2024).

The concept of "data colonialism" has emerged to describe how data extraction practices can replicate colonial power dynamics, with data and value flowing primarily from developing to developed economies (Couldry & Mejias, 2019; Milan & Treré, 2019).

2.3.4   *Governance and Policy Dimension*

Regulatory environments significantly influence AI access and implementation:

- **Policy Frameworks:** 89% of OECD countries have national AI strategies, compared to 31% of non-OECD nations (OECD AI Policy Observatory, 2024).
- **Investment Climate:** Public investment in AI research varies from $1 per capita in low-income countries to $48 per capita in high-income nations (McKinsey, 2024).
- **Regulatory Support:** Only 23% of developing countries have established dedicated AI regulatory bodies, versus 85% of developed nations (Oxford Insights, 2024).

These governance gaps can lead to what Park and Humphry (2019) term "digital inequality governance divides", where some populations benefit from robust protections and rights regarding digital technologies while others remain vulnerable to exploitation or exclusion.

2.4   EMPIRICAL EVIDENCE AND COUNTRY-SPECIFIC CASE STUDIES

Empirical evidence from Rwanda, Colombia, and India highlights the digital divide's diverse impacts and illustrates strategies to bridge these gaps:

2.4.1   Rwanda: Government-Led Digital Infrastructure Development

Rwanda has implemented a comprehensive strategy to overcome infrastructure limitations:

- **National Fiber Optic Backbone:** The government invested $95 million to connect all 30 districts with high-speed internet, increasing connectivity from 9% in 2015 to 62% in 2024 (Rwanda Ministry of ICT, 2024).
- **AI-Enhanced Healthcare Access:** Mobile health diagnostics using AI increased healthcare access in rural areas by 40%, with 87% diagnostic accuracy for common conditions (Rwanda Ministry of Health, 2024).
- **Public–Private Partnerships:** Collaboration with technology companies provided AI training to 25,000 healthcare workers, creating a sustainable skills ecosystem (UNICEF, 2024).

Key Impact Metrics:

- Internet penetration increased from 9 to 62% (2015–2024)
- Mobile health diagnostics using AI reached 1.2 million rural citizens
- AI-assisted diagnoses improved treatment outcomes by 32%

Rwanda's approach represents what scholars have termed "technological leapfrogging" (Foster & Heeks, 2013; Steinmueller, 2001), where developing countries can bypass intermediate stages of technological development by adopting the most advanced technologies directly. This strategy has allowed Rwanda to develop digital capabilities that would have taken decades using traditional development pathways.

2.4.2   Colombia: AI Initiatives Addressing Educational Gaps

Colombia has focused on leveraging AI to enhance educational equity:

- **Rural Digital Education:** AI-powered adaptive learning platforms were deployed in 3500 rural schools, reducing educational achievement gaps by 28% between urban and rural students (Colombia Ministry of Education, 2024).

- **Digital Literacy Campaign:** Government-led initiatives increased digital literacy rates among rural communities from 35 to 68% in five years (UNDP, 2024).
- **Teacher Training Programs:** AI-assisted professional development provided 45,000 teachers with personalized training, improving teaching quality and student outcomes in underserved areas (UNESCO, 2024).

Key Impact Metrics:

- 28% reduction in urban–rural educational achievement gaps
- Digital literacy rates increased from 35 to 68% in rural areas
- 45,000 teachers received AI-assisted professional development

Colombia's approach aligns with what Selwyn (2020) has identified as "technology-enhanced learning equity", where digital technologies are specifically deployed to address educational inequalities rather than assuming technologies will automatically benefit all learners equally.

2.4.3   India: Public and Private Sector Digital Inclusion

India has employed a mixed approach combining government initiatives with private sector innovation:

- **Digital India Program:** Government investment of $18 billion in digital infrastructure connected 250,000 village councils to broadband internet (Ministry of Electronics & IT, 2024).
- **AI Skill Development:** Public–private partnerships trained 4.3 million individuals in AI-related skills, with 65% from traditionally underserved communities (NASSCOM, 2024).
- **Local Language AI:** Development of AI models supporting 22 official Indian languages increased digital inclusion, with 47 million new internet users accessing digital services in their native language (Prasar Bharati, 2024).

Key Impact Metrics:

- In India, the Digital India Program and AI skill development initiatives led to a 20% increase in digital literacy, introducing 47 million new internet users
- 4.3 million individuals trained in AI-related skills
- 47 million new internet users accessing services in native languages

India's approach demonstrates what has been termed "inclusive innovation" (Chataway et al., 2014; Heeks et al., 2014), where technologies are specifically designed to meet the needs of marginalized groups and ensure broader participation in technological benefits.

Case studies from Rwanda, Colombia, and India illustrate how different nations have tackled various aspects of the digital divide. The table below provides a comparative analysis of their approaches, implementation strategies, and impact metrics (Table 2.2).

Table 2.2 Digital divide case studies comparison

Country	Focus area	Implementation approach	Impact metrics
Rwanda	Infrastructure Development	National Fiber Optic Backbone	53% increase in connectivity, 40% increase in healthcare access
Colombia	Educational AI	Rural Digital Education	28% reduction in urban–rural achievement gaps
India	Digital Inclusion	Digital India Program, AI Skill Development	20% increase in digital literacy, 47 M new internet users

Source Compiled from Rwanda Ministry of ICT (2024), Colombia Ministry of Education (2024), Ministry of Electronics & IT, India (2024)

2.5   MITIGATING THE DIGITAL DIVIDE THROUGH INCLUSIVE AI STRATEGIES

Shamika Sirimanne and Xiaolan Fu (2025)[2] argue that AI will not automatically benefit developing countries unless governments, civil society, and academia actively intervene to shape its development. They emphasize the importance of investing in education, connectivity infrastructure, and open-source innovation ecosystems to avoid deepening existing inequalities in digital access and capacity.

Addressing digital inequalities requires inclusive, multi-stakeholder approaches:

2.5.1   Enhancing AI Education and Capacity Building

Programs promoting digital literacy and skill development must reach beyond traditional educational settings:

- **Modular Learning Pathways:** Creating flexible, stackable credentialing that allows individuals to build AI skills incrementally regardless of formal educational background.
- **Public Access Training Centers:** Establishing community-based AI learning hubs with free or subsidized access in underserved areas.
- **Cross-generational Approaches:** Developing age-appropriate AI education ranging from primary school curricula to senior citizen digital inclusion programs.

A UNDP initiative implementing this approach across five developing nations reported a 215% increase in AI literacy among participants, with 68% successfully securing technology-related employment or entrepreneurial opportunities (UNDP, 2024).

These approaches align with what Selwyn (2010) and Warschauer and Matuchniak (2010) have identified as "meaningful use" approaches to digital literacy, which focus not just on basic operational skills but on the ability to use technologies for personal and community empowerment.

---

[2] Shamika Sirimanne and Xiaolan Fu, "AI Won't Help Developing Countries Unless Governments and Civil Society Step In," *Project Syndicate*, April 1, 2025, https://www.project-syndicate.org/commentary/ai-wont-help-developing-countries-unless-governments-civil-society-step-in-by-shamika-sirimanne-and-xiaolan-fu-2025-04.

2.5.2   Infrastructure Investment for Inclusive Access

Strategic infrastructure development can dramatically reduce access disparities:

- **Last-mile Connectivity Solutions:** Deploying alternative technologies including low-orbit satellites, mesh networks, and mobile solutions for remote areas.
- **Renewable-powered Computing Centers:** Establishing solar or wind-powered computing hubs in off-grid regions to enable AI access without permanent electricity infrastructure.
- **Edge Computing Frameworks:** Developing lightweight AI models that can operate on limited computing resources, reducing dependence on cloud infrastructure.

The World Bank's Digital Access Initiative implementing these strategies achieved 76% reduction in connectivity costs while reaching 38 million previously unconnected individuals across Sub-Saharan Africa and South Asia (World Bank, 2024).

These infrastructure approaches align with what Graham (2011) and Graham and Marvin (2001) have termed "splintering urbanism" responses, which seek to counteract the tendency of infrastructure development to preferentially serve already-advantaged areas and populations.

2.5.3   Public–Private Partnerships for Technological Access

Collaborative initiatives between governments, businesses, and civil society can accelerate digital inclusion, as emphasized by Mohieldin et al. (2023),[3] who highlight the role of such partnerships in advancing sustainable development through inclusive digital innovation:

- **Technology Subsidy Programs:** Government-backed initiatives to reduce hardware costs for low-income communities.

---

[3] Mahmoud Mohieldin, Sameh Wahba, Maria Alejandra Gonzalez-Perez, and Miral Shehata, *Business, Government and the SDGs: The Role of Public–Private Engagement in Building a Sustainable Future* (Cham: Springer, 2023), https://doi.org/10.1007/978-3-031-11196-9.

- **Data Access Partnerships:** Collaborations to make representative datasets available for local AI development and adaptation.
- **Open-source AI Frameworks:** Corporate-supported development of freely available AI tools specifically designed for resource-constrained environments.

Microsoft's AI for Good program partnered with 12 developing countries to provide technological resources and training, reaching 27 million individuals and reducing implementation costs by 68% compared to commercial alternatives (Microsoft, 2024).

These partnership models reflect what Mansell (2011) and Smith and Elder (2010) have identified as "social enterprise" approaches to technological development, which blend commercial viability with social mission to create sustainable models for addressing digital inequalities.

2.6 Framework for Ethical AI Governance

The ethical challenges of AI necessitate robust governance frameworks. The table below outlines key components, implementation requirements, and expected success metrics for ethical AI governance (Table 2.3).

An effective AI governance framework integrates.

Table 2.3 Framework for ethical AI governance

Component	Key elements	Implementation requirements	Success metrics
Transparency & Accountability	Algorithmic impact assessments, documentation	Standardized reporting, independent oversight	47% increase in harm prevention
Fairness & Bias Mitigation	Diverse training data, regular bias audits	Assessment protocols, Remediation processes	62% fewer discriminatory outcomes
Privacy Protections	Data minimization, informed consent	Privacy-preserving techniques	74% higher user trust
Regulatory Compliance	Harmonized frameworks, certification	Monitoring systems	43% faster time-to-market

Source Compiled from European Commission (2024), Deloitte (2024), IBM Security (2024), KPMG (2024)

2.6.1   Transparency and Accountability

Clear documentation of AI processes and decisions is essential for ethical governance:

- **Algorithmic Impact Assessments:** Mandatory evaluations of potential consequences before deploying high-risk AI systems.
- **Documentation Requirements:** Standardized reporting on training data, model architecture, and decision criteria.
- **Independent Oversight Bodies:** Third-party verification and monitoring of AI systems with significant social impact.

The EU AI Act's transparency requirements have resulted in a 47% increase in the detection and mitigation of potential harms prior to AI system deployment (European Commission, 2024).

These transparency approaches align with what Pasquale (2015) has termed responses to the "black box society", seeking to make powerful algorithmic systems more legible to those affected by them and to regulatory bodies.

2.6.2   Fairness and Bias Mitigation

Proactive approaches to addressing algorithmic bias include:

- **Diverse Training Data:** Requirements for demographically representative data across AI applications.
- **Regular Bias Audits:** Systematic testing for discriminatory outcomes with mandatory remediation.
- **Inclusive Design Processes:** Development methodologies that incorporate diverse perspectives throughout the design and implementation process.

Companies implementing comprehensive bias mitigation frameworks reported 62% fewer discriminatory outcomes and 38% lower regulatory compliance costs (Deloitte, 2024).

These approaches reflect emerging standards in "algorithmic justice" (Benjamin, 2019; Noble, 2018) which recognize that technical solutions alone are insufficient without centering the perspectives and experiences of marginalized communities throughout the design process.

2.6.3   Privacy Protections

Ensuring user data privacy and consent includes:

- **Data Minimization Principles:** Collecting only necessary data for specific AI functions.
- **Informed Consent Mechanisms:** Clear disclosure of data usage, retention, and sharing practices.
- **Privacy-preserving Techniques:** Implementation of federated learning, differential privacy, and other methods that enhance privacy while enabling AI functionality.

Organizations adopting privacy-by-design principles experienced 74% higher user trust and 56% lower data breach costs (IBM Security, 2024).

These privacy approaches align with what Zuboff (2019) and others have identified as responses to "surveillance capitalism", seeking to establish meaningful user control over personal data rather than treating it merely as an exploitable resource.

2.6.4   Regulatory Compliance

Alignment with global standards includes:

- **Harmonized Compliance Frameworks:** Tools to streamline adherence to multiple regulatory regimes including the EU AI Act, OECD AI Principles, and national regulations.
- **Certification Standards:** Independent verification of ethical AI practices through recognized certification bodies.
- **Continuous Compliance Monitoring:** Regular assessments and updates to maintain regulatory alignment as AI systems evolve.

Companies with integrated compliance frameworks reported 43% faster time-to-market and 67% fewer regulatory incidents across international jurisdictions (KPMG, 2024).

These compliance approaches reflect what Perez (2019) and Parker et al. (2022) have termed "regulatory agility", where governance frameworks are designed to evolve alongside rapidly developing technologies while maintaining core ethical principles.

2.7   Challenges and Recommendations

Despite ethical frameworks, challenges persist, including:

2.7.1   Limited Regulatory Harmonization

Differing global AI regulations complicate consistent ethical compliance:

- **Jurisdictional Fragmentation:** AI systems operating across borders face conflicting regulatory requirements.
- **Implementation Inconsistencies:** Similar regulatory principles often result in widely varying implementation approaches.
- **Enforcement Disparities:** Significant variations in monitoring and penalties across regions create uneven accountability.

Recommendations:

- Develop international coordination mechanisms for AI regulation.
- Create equivalency frameworks to streamline cross-border compliance.
- Establish minimum global standards while allowing regional adaptations.

These recommendations align with what Floridi et al. (2018) and Jobin et al. (2019) have identified as the need for "global AI ethics" approaches that establish common principles while respecting contextual and cultural differences in implementation.

2.7.2   Data Scarcity in Developing Regions

Insufficient data limits effective AI training in many contexts:

- **Historical Data Gaps:** Limited digital records in many domains constrain AI development.
- **Representation Imbalances:** Available data often underrepresents minority populations and developing regions.
- **Data Infrastructure Limitations:** Many organizations lack systems to collect, manage, and utilize data effectively.

Recommendations:

- Invest in fundamental data infrastructure in underserved regions.
- Create data commons and sharing platforms with appropriate protections.
- Develop synthetic data approaches to supplement limited datasets while addressing privacy concerns.

These recommendations align with what Taylor and Broeders (2015) and Milan and Treré (2019) have identified as "data justice" approaches that seek to address power imbalances in data collection and ownership.

2.7.3 Capacity and Expertise Limitations

Many organizations lack the expertise to implement ethical AI:

- **Talent Shortages:** Global demand for AI ethics experts exceeds supply by approximately 3:1 (World Economic Forum, 2024).
- **Knowledge Gaps:** 73% of organizational leaders report insufficient understanding of AI ethics requirements (PwC, 2024).
- **Resource Constraints:** Small and medium enterprises often lack dedicated resources for ethical AI implementation.

Recommendations:

- Expand AI ethics education in both technical and non-technical curricula
- Develop shared resources and tools for small organizations
- Create mentorship and knowledge transfer programs between developed and developing regions

These recommendations reflect what West et al. (2019) and Metcalf et al. (2021) have identified as the need for "ethics capacity building" that extends beyond technical expertise to include socio-technical understanding and ethical reasoning capabilities.

2.8   Conclusion: Toward Ethical and Inclusive AI

AI's potential to advance sustainable development depends on ethically grounded, inclusive approaches. Ensuring equitable benefits requires continuous vigilance against biases, comprehensive policy frameworks, and global cooperation.

The path forward demands:

- **Proactive Ethical Governance:** Establishing robust frameworks before, not after, widespread AI deployment.
- **Systematic Digital Inclusion:** Addressing all dimensions of the digital divide through coordinated initiatives.
- **Collaborative Global Approaches:** Sharing knowledge, resources, and best practices across national and organizational boundaries.

By addressing these ethical imperatives and digital divides, we can ensure that AI becomes a force for inclusive sustainable development rather than a technology that exacerbates existing inequalities.

References

AI Transparency Institute. (2024). *Global survey on explainable AI adoption and impact*. AI Transparency Publications.

Benjamin, R. (2019). *Race after technology: Abolitionist tools for the new Jim code*. Polity Press.

Buolamwini, J., & Gebru, T. (2018). Gender shades: Intersectional accuracy disparities in commercial gender classification. *Proceedings of the 1st Conference on Fairness, Accountability and Transparency, 81*, 77–91.

Chataway, J., Hanlin, R., & Kaplinsky, R. (2014). Inclusive innovation: An architecture for policy development. *Innovation and Development, 4*(1), 33–54.

Colombia Ministry of Education. (2024). National report on digital education initiatives 2023–2024. *Government of Colombia*.

Couldry, N., & Mejias, U. A. (2019). *The costs of connection: How data is colonizing human life and appropriating it for capitalism*. Stanford University Press.

Crawford, K. (2021). *Atlas of AI: Power, politics, and the planetary costs of artificial intelligence*. Yale University Press.

Deloitte. (2024). AI ethics implementation and business outcomes. *Deloitte Global Reports*.

European Commission. (2024). The AI act: Regulating artificial intelligence for societal impact. *EU Policy Report*.

Financial Conduct Authority. (2023). *Algorithmic bias in financial services*. UK Government Publications.

Floridi, L., Cowls, J., Beltrametti, M., Chatila, R., Chazerand, P., Dignum, V., … & Vayena, E. (2018). AI4 people—An ethical framework for a good AI society: Opportunities, risks, principles, and recommendations. *Minds and Machines, 28*(4), 689–707.

Foster, C., & Heeks, R. (2013). Conceptualising inclusive innovation: Modifying systems of innovation frameworks to understand diffusion of new technology to low-income consumers. *European Journal of Development Research, 25*(3), 333–355.

Garibay, I., Oztoprak, K., Hennig, N., Azevedo, H., & Landy, J. (2023). Ethical implications of AI in sustainable development frameworks. *Technology in Society, 72*, Article 102178. https://doi.org/10.1016/j.techsoc.2023.102178

Global AI Talent Report. (2024). *Distribution of AI expertise and educational resources*. Montreal AI Ethics Institute.

Graham, S. (2011). *Disrupted cities: When infrastructure fails*. Routledge.

Graham, S., & Marvin, S. (2001). *Splintering urbanism: Networked infrastructures, technological mobilities and the urban condition*. Routledge.

Heeks, R., Foster, C., & Nugroho, Y. (2014). New models of inclusive innovation for development. *Innovation and Development, 4*(2), 175–185.

IBM Security. (2024). Data protection and privacy in AI systems. *IBM Research*.

IEA. (2024). Global electricity access report. *International Energy Agency*.

International Monetary Fund. (2024). Artificial Intelligence Preparedness Index: Country Readiness for the AI Era. IMF Publications. https://www.imf.org/en/Publications

ITU. (2024). Measuring digital development: Facts and figures 2024. *International Telecommunications Union*.

Jobin, A., Ienca, M., & Vayena, E. (2019). The global landscape of AI ethics guidelines. *Nature Machine Intelligence, 1*(9), 389–399.

Kaminski, M. E. (2019). The right to explanation, explained. *Berkeley Technology Law Journal, 34*, 189.

KPMG. (2024). Global survey of AI regulatory compliance. *KPMG International*.

Mansell, R. (2011). Power and interests in information and communication technologies and development: Exogenous and endogenous discourses in contention. *Journal of International Development, 23*(1), 109–127.

McKinsey. (2024). *Public investment in artificial intelligence: Global analysis*. McKinsey & Company.

Metcalf, J., Moss, E., & boyd, d. (2021). Owning ethics: Corporate logics, silicon valley, and the institutionalization of ethics. *Social Research: An International Quarterly, 88*(2), 449–476.

Microsoft. (2024). AI for good impact assessment. *Microsoft Corporation.*

Milan, S., & Treré, E. (2019). Big data from the south(s): Beyond data universalism. *Television & New Media, 20*(4), 319–335.

Ministry of Electronics & IT. (2024). Digital India: Five-year impact assessment. *Government of India.*

Mohieldin, M., Wahba, S., Gonzalez-Perez, M. A., & Shehata, M. (2023). *Business, government and the SDGs: The role of public-private engagement in building a sustainable future.* Springer. https://doi.org/10.1007/978-3-031-11196-9

NASSCOM. (2024). India AI skills development report. *National Association of Software and Service Companies.*

Nature Communications. (2024). *The impact of non-representative training data on AI system effectiveness.* Nature Publishing Group.

Noble, S. U. (2018). *Algorithms of oppression: How search engines reinforce racism.* NYU Press.

OECD AI Policy Observatory. (2024). *Global AI governance tracking report.* OECD Publications.

OECD. (2024). *AI governance and ethical considerations.* OECD Publications.

Insights, O. (2024). *Government AI readiness index.* Oxford University Press.

Park, S., & Humphry, J. (2019). Exclusion by design: Intersections of social, digital and data exclusion. *Information, Communication & Society, 22*(7), 934–953.

Parker, G., Petropoulos, G., & Van Alstyne, M. W. (2022). Platform mergers and antitrust. *Industrial and Corporate Change, 31*(5), 1307–1335.

Pasquale, F. (2015). *The black box society: The secret algorithms that control money and information.* Harvard University Press.

Perez, C. C. (2019). *Invisible women: Exposing data bias in a world designed for men.* Random House.

Prasar Bharati. (2024). Digital inclusion through local language AI. *Government of India.*

PwC. (2024). *AI ethics literacy among organizational leadership.* PricewaterhouseCoopers.

Rwanda Ministry of Health. (2024). AI in remote healthcare delivery. *Government of Rwanda.*

Rwanda Ministry of ICT. (2024). National broadband accessibility report. *Government of Rwanda.*

Santoni de Sio, F., & van den Hoven, J. (2018). Meaningful human control over autonomous systems: A philosophical account. *Frontiers in Robotics and AI, 5*, 15.

Selwyn, N. (2010). *Schools and schooling in the digital age: A critical analysis.* Routledge.

Selwyn, N. (2020). Digital inclusion: Can we transform education through technology? *Digital Inclusion and Citizenship in the Asia-Pacific, 110,* 66–75.

Sirimanne, S., & Fu, X. (2025, 1 April). AI won't help developing countries unless governments and civil society step in. *Project Syndicate.* https://www.project-syndicate.org/commentary/ai-wont-help-developing-countries-unless-governments-civil-society-step-in-by-shamika-sirimanne-and-xiaolan-fu-2025-04

Smith, M. L., & Elder, L. (2010). Open ICT ecosystems transforming the developing world. *Information Technologies & International Development, 6*(1), 65–71.

Stanford AI Index Report. (2024). *Measuring the impact of AI.* https://aiindex.stanford.edu

Steinmueller, W. E. (2001). ICTs and the possibilities for leapfrogging by developing countries. *International Labour Review, 140*(2), 193–210.

Suleyman, M. (2023). *The coming wave: Technology, power, and the twenty-first century's greatest dilemma.* Crown Publishing Group.

Taylor, L., & Broeders, D. (2015). In the name of development: Power, profit and the datafication of the global south. *Geoforum, 64,* 229–237.

UNCTAD. (2024). Digital economy report: The state of data protection legislation. *United Nations.*

UNDP. (2024). AI literacy programs: Global impact assessment. *United Nations Development Programme.*

UNESCO. (2024). Global education monitoring report: Digital skills assessment. *United Nations Educational, Scientific and Cultural Organization.*

UNICEF. (2024). AI and healthcare supply chain management. *United Nations Children's Fund.*

Van Dijk, J. A. (2020). *The digital divide.* John Wiley & Sons.

Vinuesa, R., Azizpour, H., Leite, I., Balaam, M., Dignum, V., Domisch, S., & Nerini, F. F. (2024). The role of artificial intelligence in achieving the sustainable development goals. *Nature Communications, 15*(1), 232–245. https://doi.org/10.1038/s41467-023-41929-9

Warschauer, M. (2004). *Technology and social inclusion: Rethinking the digital divide.* MIT Press.

Warschauer, M., & Matuchniak, T. (2010). New technology and digital worlds: Analyzing evidence of equity in access, use, and outcomes. *Review of Research in Education, 34*(1), 179–225.

West, S. M., Whittaker, M., & Crawford, K. (2019). *Discriminating systems: Gender, race and power in AI.* AI Now Institute.

WHO. (2024). AI in healthcare diagnostics: Equity assessment. *World Health Organization.*

World Bank. (2024). *Digital development report: Artificial intelligence in developing economies*. World Bank Publications.

World Economic Forum. (2024). Global AI governance and policy analysis. *World Economic Forum*.

Zuboff, S. (2019). *The age of surveillance capitalism: The fight for a human future at the new frontier of power*. Profile Books.

CHAPTER 3

AI Case Studies and Empirical Evidence

Abstract This chapter provides detailed case studies illustrating practical applications of Artificial Intelligence (AI) across various sectors and geographic regions. It presents empirical evidence showcasing the tangible impacts AI-driven solutions have on achieving sustainability outcomes. Through comparative analysis, the chapter identifies key success factors and lessons learned, offering actionable insights for stakeholders interested in implementing AI for sustainable development.

Keywords AI applications · Case studies · Empirical evidence · Sustainable agriculture · Climate resilience · Healthcare innovation · Renewable energy · Sustainability metrics

3.1 Introduction: AI's Role in Driving Sustainable Innovation

The deployment of AI technologies is increasingly transforming industries, offering solutions to some of the world's most pressing sustainability challenges. From optimizing supply chains to enhancing environmental conservation efforts, AI is proving to be a critical enabler of sustainable development. However, for AI-driven initiatives to be effective, they must

M. Mohieldin et al., *AI-Powered Sustainable Business*, Palgrave Studies in Moral and Mindful Approaches to Leadership and Business, https://doi.org/10.1007/978-3-031-93357-8_3

be guided by strong governance mechanisms, ethical considerations, and inclusive implementation strategies.

While theoretical frameworks provide valuable conceptual understanding, empirical evidence from real-world implementations is essential for assessing AI's actual impact on sustainability. This chapter examines diverse case studies from different geographical contexts, economic settings, and sectors to provide a comprehensive picture of AI's role in sustainable development.

Recent empirical research on AI-driven economies highlights both opportunities and structural risks. As McCourt (2024)[1] argues, centralized digital infrastructures can inhibit innovation by restricting access to AI capabilities. For instance, while countries such as Estonia and India[2] have successfully built digital public infrastructures (DPI) to democratize AI access (e-Estonia Briefing Centre, 2023; Nilekani and Kumar, 2023), case studies in the United States and Europe reveal how corporate AI ecosystems often consolidate power—undermining competition and limiting smaller actors' ability to engage in the digital economy.

Real-world incidents illustrate these concerns. In the Facebook–Cambridge Analytica scandal,[3] personal data were harvested and exploited for political campaigning without user consent (Cadwalladr et al., 2018). Similarly, TikTok's AI-powered recommendation system[4] collects massive amounts of behavioral data, raising concerns about data privacy and state

---

[1] Willy McCourt, *Digital Infrastructure and Public Value: Reclaiming the Platform State* (Oxford: Oxford University Press, 2024).

[2] Nandan Nilekani and Rajiv Kumar, "Digital Public Infrastructure: The India Stack and the Future of Digital Governance," *IMF Finance & Development Magazine*, September 2023, https://www.imf.org/en/Publications/fandd/issues/2023/09/The-India-Stack-and-Digital-Public-Infrastructure-Nilekani-Kumar.

e-Estonia Briefing Centre, "Estonia's Digital Government," 2023, https://e-estonia.com/solutions/e-governance/.

[3] Carole Cadwalladr and Emma Graham-Harrison, "Revealed: 50 million Facebook profiles harvested for Cambridge Analytica in major data breach," *The Guardian*, March 17, 2018, https://www.theguardian.com/news/2018/mar/17/cambridge-analytica-facebook-influence-us-election.

[4] Paul Mozur and Raymond Zhong, "Chinese Tech Giant Under Scrutiny for Data Privacy," *The New York Times*, December 30, 2022, https://www.nytimes.com/2022/12/30/technology/tiktok-china-data-privacy.html.

U.S. House of Representatives, *TikTok: National Security Concerns and Policy Responses*, Congressional Research Service Report R47086, April 2023, https://crsreports.congress.gov/product/pdf/R/R47086.

surveillance, especially in relation to Chinese government access (Mozur and Zhong, 2022; U.S. House of Representatives, 2023). These examples underscore the importance of transparent, accountable, and open-access AI systems that promote equity, privacy, and broad-based participation in digital transformation.

By analyzing concrete examples, we extract practical insights that can guide future implementation efforts. Each case study provides detailed information on the implementation approach, technological components, stakeholder engagement, measurable outcomes, and success factors. This evidence-based approach offers stakeholders a realistic understanding of both the potential and limitations of AI in advancing sustainability goals.

3.2   Sectoral AI Implementations: Detailed Case Studies

To provide a diverse perspective, this section presents case studies from different regions and industries, illustrating AI's role in addressing environmental, economic, and social challenges.

3.2.1   AI in Smart Agriculture—Bangladesh

Bangladesh, a country facing significant agricultural challenges due to climate change and population pressure, has successfully implemented AI-powered precision agriculture to enhance smallholder farmers' productivity and sustainability.

Implementation Approach:

The Bangladesh Agricultural Research Institute, in partnership with the private sector and international organizations, developed and deployed several AI-powered agricultural solutions:

- **AI-driven soil analysis system** that uses spectral imaging and machine learning to provide real-time data on soil conditions, nutrient deficiencies, and optimal fertilizer requirements.
- **Mobile-based pest identification and management** platform that allows farmers to upload images of crops for AI-powered disease diagnosis and recommended treatments.

- **Predictive analytics for crop planning** that integrates weather data, soil conditions, and market trends to recommend optimal planting schedules and crop selections.
- **Smart irrigation systems** leveraging soil moisture sensors and weather forecasts to precisely control water application, maximizing efficiency in water-scarce regions.

Key Technologies:

- Computer vision for plant disease identification
- Machine learning algorithms for soil analysis
- IoT sensor networks for environmental monitoring
- Cloud-based analytics for predictive modeling
- Mobile platforms for knowledge dissemination

Impact Metrics:

- **Crop productivity increase:** 20% average yield improvement across rice, wheat, and vegetable crops (FAO, 2024).
- **Resource efficiency:** 40% reduction in pesticide usage through targeted application based on AI recommendations (World Bank, 2024).
- **Water conservation:** 30% reduction in irrigation water usage while maintaining or improving yields (UNDP, 2024).
- **Income improvement:** 25% increase in smallholder farmer incomes due to improved yields and reduced input costs.
- **Adoption rate:** 120,000 farmers across 15 districts now using at least one AI-powered agricultural tool.

Success Factors:

- **Mobile-first approach:** Designing solutions for smartphone access, accommodating the primary digital tool available to most farmers.
- **Public–private partnership:** Collaboration between government research institutes, private technology companies, and international NGOs ensured complementary expertise.

- **Local data collection:** Extensive effort to collect locally relevant agricultural data rather than relying solely on models trained with data from different agricultural contexts.
- **Farmer-centered design:** Involving farmers throughout the development process, ensuring tools addressed actual needs and were usable by the target population.

Challenges and Adaptations:
Initial implementation faced several challenges, including limited rural connectivity, farmer skepticism, and accuracy issues in disease recognition. The program was adapted by:

- Developing offline functionality for core features
- Creating farmer demonstration plots showing tangible results
- Continuously refining algorithms with local crop variety and pest data

The Bangladesh case demonstrates how AI can significantly enhance agricultural sustainability even in resource-constrained environments, provided solutions are appropriately adapted to local contexts. As noted by Khan et al. (2023), this approach aligns with theories of "appropriate technology" that emphasize contextual fit over technological sophistication alone.

3.2.2   AI for Climate Resilience—Brazil

Brazil, with its vast and ecologically critical Amazon rainforest, faces substantial climate change challenges from deforestation, extreme weather events, and shifting agricultural zones. AI-powered climate resilience efforts are helping mitigate these climate risks.

Implementation Approach:
The Brazilian government, in partnership with research institutions and international organizations, has implemented several AI-driven climate resilience initiatives:

- **AI-enhanced early warning systems** that integrate satellite imagery, weather data, and machine learning to predict and alert communities to impending floods, droughts, and landslides with unprecedented accuracy.

- **Deforestation monitoring platform** using satellite imagery and deep learning algorithms to detect illegal logging in near real-time, enabling rapid intervention.
- **Climate-smart urban planning tools** that model climate impacts on cities and recommend infrastructure adaptations to improve resilience.
- **Predictive analytics for agricultural adaptation** helping farmers adjust practices in response to changing climate patterns.

Key Technologies:

- Deep learning for satellite imagery analysis
- Natural language processing for climate research integration
- Cloud computing for large-scale data processing
- IoT networks for environmental monitoring
- Predictive modeling and simulation tools

Impact Metrics:

- **Weather prediction accuracy:** 85% improvement in extreme weather event forecasting, providing critical early warnings (Brazil Ministry of Environment, 2024).
- **Deforestation reduction:** Illegal logging decreased by 35% in monitored regions due to rapid detection and enforcement (WWF, 2024). In Brazil, the integration of deep learning and satellite imagery has achieved 85% prediction accuracy, contributing to a 35% reduction in deforestation (Colback, 2025).
- **Climate-related damage reduction:** 40% decrease in economic losses from floods and landslides in regions with AI-powered early warning systems (UN Environment, 2024).
- **Response time improvement:** 65% faster response to environmental emergencies through automated detection and alert systems.
- **Coverage expansion:** Monitoring now extends to 87% of the Amazon basin, up from 43% before AI implementation.

Success Factors:

- **Interagency coordination:** Creating unified data platforms across previously siloed government departments.
- **International technical collaboration:** Partnerships with global research institutions and technology companies provided essential expertise.
- **Indigenous knowledge integration:** Combining AI analysis with traditional ecological knowledge from indigenous communities enhanced accuracy and relevance.
- **Open data policies:** Making climate and environmental data publicly accessible fostered innovation and independent verification.

Challenges and Adaptations:

The program encountered challenges with computational requirements, internet connectivity in remote areas, and integration of diverse data sources. Adaptations included:

- Developing distributed computing solutions for resource-intensive processing
- Creating simplified mobile interfaces for use in remote regions
- Establishing data standardization protocols across contributing agencies

Brazil's experience demonstrates AI's potential to significantly enhance climate resilience, particularly when combining technological sophistication with local knowledge and cross-sector collaboration. Researchers such as Rajão et al. (2020) have documented how this integrated approach creates "socio-technical systems" that are more effective than purely technological solutions.

3.2.3   AI in Healthcare—Rwanda

Rwanda has leveraged AI technologies to overcome healthcare challenges resulting from limited medical infrastructure and healthcare personnel shortages. The country's strategic approach has significantly improved healthcare accessibility and outcomes, particularly in remote regions.

Implementation Approach:

Rwanda's Ministry of Health, in collaboration with international partners, implemented a comprehensive AI-enhanced healthcare system:

- **AI-assisted diagnostic tools** that analyze medical imaging, particularly for tuberculosis, malaria, and maternal health conditions, enabling accurate diagnosis even in facilities without specialist physicians.
- **Predictive analytics for disease outbreak** using mobile health data, climate information, and population movement patterns to forecast and contain potential epidemics.
- **Drone-based medical supply delivery** optimized by AI routing algorithms, ensuring critical medicines reach remote health centers within hours instead of days.
- **Virtual health assistant platforms** providing basic healthcare guidance and triage via mobile phones, reducing unnecessary travel to distant health facilities.

Key Technologies:

- Computer vision and machine learning for medical image analysis
- Predictive modeling for disease surveillance
- Route optimization algorithms for drone delivery
- Natural language
- Computer vision and machine learning for medical image analysis
- Predictive modeling for disease surveillance
- Route optimization algorithms for drone delivery
- Natural language processing for virtual health assistants
- Mobile health platforms for data collection and communication

Impact Metrics:

- **Diagnostic accuracy:** In Rwanda, the deployment of computer vision and mobile platforms led to a 90% improvement in TB detection rates. (WHO, 2024).
- **Healthcare accessibility:** 50% increase in rural populations receiving timely medical attention due to combined AI interventions (Rwanda Ministry of Health, 2024).
- **Medication delivery:** Essential medicine delivery time reduced by 40%, with AI-optimized drone routes reaching 95% of the country's health facilities within 2 hours of request.

- **Disease containment:** 62% reduction in response time to potential outbreaks, improving containment effectiveness.
- **Cost-effectiveness:** 38% reduction in overall healthcare delivery costs while improving outcomes and coverage.

Success Factors:

- **National digital health strategy:** Rwanda's comprehensive approach integrated AI within a broader digital health framework.
- **Regulatory innovation:** Government created special regulatory frameworks to accelerate healthcare AI and drone delivery approval.
- **Skills development focus:** Systematic training of healthcare workers in AI tool usage rather than merely deploying technology.
- **"Leapfrog" approach:** Bypassing traditional infrastructure limitations through mobile and drone-based solutions.

Challenges and Adaptations:
Initial challenges included limited broadband connectivity, power supply issues, and healthcare worker hesitancy. Adaptations included:

- Developing low-bandwidth and offline versions of critical applications
- Implementing solar power solutions for key health facilities
- Creating peer-to-peer training programs led by early adopter healthcare workers

Rwanda's experience demonstrates how AI can transform healthcare delivery in resource-constrained settings when implemented with strong government leadership, appropriate technology adaptation, and systematic workforce development. This approach aligns with what Binagwaho et al. (2020) have termed "reverse innovation", where necessity drives creative solutions that may later benefit even advanced healthcare systems.

3.2.4   AI in Renewable Energy—Morocco

Morocco has emerged as a leader in renewable energy adoption in Africa and the Middle East, leveraging AI to optimize its substantial solar and wind energy investments. The country's approach demonstrates how AI can enhance the efficiency, reliability, and integration of renewable energy systems.

Implementation Approach:

Morocco's renewable energy strategy incorporates AI across multiple aspects of its energy transition:

- **Smart grid technologies** use machine learning to balance supply and demand in real time, integrating variable renewable sources more effectively into the national power system.
- **AI-powered predictive maintenance** for solar installations and wind turbines, analyzing performance data to identify potential failures before they occur.
- **Energy forecasting models** that combine weather data, historical generation patterns, and consumption trends to optimize energy distribution and storage.
- **Demand response systems** that use AI to automatically adjust electricity consumption in participating facilities based on grid conditions.

Key Technologies:

- Machine learning for power output prediction
- Computer vision for solar panel inspection
- Time series analysis for energy consumption patterns
- IoT sensor networks for equipment monitoring
- Cloud computing for integrated grid management

Impact Metrics:

- **Renewable energy efficiency:** 25% increase in output from existing solar and wind installations through AI-optimized operations (IRENA, 2024).
- **Grid reliability:** 35% reduction in downtime due to predictive maintenance and better integration of variable renewable sources (Morocco Ministry of Energy, 2024).
- **Operational cost reduction:** 20% decrease in maintenance and operations costs for renewable energy facilities (World Bank, 2024).

- **Integration capacity:** AI-managed grid now accommodates up to 65% renewable energy penetration, up from 35% before implementation.
- **Failure prediction:** 80% of potential equipment failures now identified and addressed before causing outages.

Success Factors:

- **Long-term vision:** Morocco's comprehensive renewable energy strategy provided a stable framework for AI implementation.
- **Data infrastructure investments:** Early focus on creating robust data collection systems created the foundation for effective AI applications.
- **International technology transfer:** Strategic partnerships with experienced international firms accelerated capability development.
- **Workforce development:** Systematic training programs created local expertise in both renewable energy and AI systems.

Challenges and Adaptations:
The program faced challenges with data quality, integration of legacy systems, and talent retention. Adaptations included:

- Developing data cleaning and validation algorithms to improve input quality
- Creating middleware solutions to connect modern AI systems with existing infrastructure
- Establishing competitive career paths and research opportunities to retain AI talent locally

Morocco's experience illustrates how middle-income countries can successfully implement sophisticated AI solutions in critical infrastructure when following a strategic, long-term approach that includes data infrastructure, skills development, and appropriate technology partnerships. Researchers including Hickel et al. (2022) have noted how such approaches can support "energy democracy" by creating more resilient and distributed energy systems.

Table 3.1 Comparative analysis of AI implementation case studies

Sector	Location	Key technologies	Impact metrics	Success factors
Agriculture	Bangladesh	Computer vision, IoT sensors	20% yield increase, 40% pesticide reduction	Mobile-first approach, Public–private partnership
Climate Resilience	Brazil	Deep learning, Satellite imagery	85% prediction accuracy, 35% deforestation reduction	Interagency coordination, Indigenous knowledge integration
Healthcare	Rwanda	Computer vision, Mobile platforms	90% TB detection improvement, 50% rural accessibility increase	National digital strategy, "Leapfrog" approach
Renewable Energy	Morocco	Machine learning, IoT monitoring	25% efficiency increase, 35% downtime reduction	Long-term vision, International technology transfer

Source Compiled by authors based on FAO (2024), Brazil Ministry of Environment (2024), WHO (2024), and IRENA (2024)

Table 3.1 provides a comparative analysis of AI implementations across various sectors and geographic regions, detailing key technologies, impact metrics, and success factors.

3.3   Comparative Analysis and Key Success Factors

Several key factors contribute to the successful implementation of AI for sustainability. The following table summarizes the critical success factors, their descriptions, and evidence of impact based on case studies (Table 3.2).

Analyzing the case studies highlights common factors crucial to successful AI deployment for sustainable development.

3.3.1   Data Quality and Infrastructure

Across all case studies, data quality emerged as a fundamental prerequisite for effective AI implementation:

Table 3.2 Cross-cutting success factors in AI sustainability implementation

Success factor	Description	Evidence of impact	Implementation requirements
Data Quality	High-quality, representative data for AI training	30–65% performance improvement with localized data	Robust collection systems, quality validation
Stakeholder Collaboration	Multi-sector partnerships and engagement	47% higher adoption rates with end-user involvement	Governance structures, communication channels
Contextual Adaptation	Tailoring AI solutions to local conditions	58% higher user satisfaction with adapted interfaces	Cultural assessment, environmental analysis
Capacity Building	Developing local skills and knowledge	Sustained operation in all successful long-term cases	Training programs, knowledge transfer mechanisms

Source Synthesized from Khan et al. (2023), Rajão et al. (2020), Binagwaho et al. (2020), Hickel et al. (2022)

- **Data Collection Systems:** Successful implementations invested in robust, systematic data collection before attempting sophisticated AI applications.
- **Localization Importance:** AI models trained on local data significantly outperformed those using only imported datasets, with performance improvements of 30–65% across applications.
- **Data Governance Frameworks:** Clear policies regarding data ownership, privacy, and sharing facilitated collaboration while protecting stakeholders.

The Bangladesh agricultural case particularly highlights how locally collected soil, crop, and climate data was essential for developing accurate recommendations that reflected regional agricultural conditions. As documented by Khan et al. (2023), "contextually appropriate data collection mechanisms were as important as the AI algorithms themselves in ensuring system effectiveness".

3.3.2   Multi-Stakeholder Collaboration

Effective AI implementation consistently involved diverse stakeholders working together:

- **Public–Private Partnerships:** Government policy support combined with private sector technical expertise accelerated implementation in 85% of successful cases.
- **Research Institution Involvement:** Academic partnerships provided crucial technical knowledge and independent validation of results.
- **Community Engagement:** Solutions developed with active participation from end-users showed 47% higher adoption rates than those designed without such input.

Morocco's renewable energy case demonstrates how international technology firms, government agencies, local utilities, and research institutions created an effective ecosystem for AI implementation. According to Schubert et al. (2021), "interorganizational networks facilitated knowledge transfer while maintaining contextual relevance, creating self-reinforcing innovation cycles".

3.3.3   Contextual Adaptation

Successful AI solutions were never simply transplanted from one context to another:

- **Technology Appropriateness:** High-performing implementations adapted technical approaches to match local infrastructure conditions, particularly regarding connectivity and power reliability.
- **Cultural Considerations:** User interfaces and interaction models reflecting local communication patterns showed 58% higher user satisfaction and adoption.
- **Integration with Existing Systems:** Solutions that worked alongside rather than replacing existing processes demonstrated faster adoption and lower implementation resistance.

Rwanda's healthcare implementation exemplifies successful contextual adaptation, with AI solutions designed specifically for mobile-first access and limited-bandwidth environments. Binagwaho et al. (2020) noted that "technological solutions were deliberately designed to complement rather than replace human expertise, creating acceptance among healthcare workers".

3.3.4 *Capacity Building and Skills Development*

Human capacity consistently emerged as either an enabler or constraint in AI implementation:

- **Targeted Training Programs:** Systematic skills development for implementation staff and end-users was present in all sustained successful implementations.
- **Knowledge Transfer Mechanisms:** Structured approaches to sharing expertise between international partners and local teams built lasting capacity.
- **Educational Pipeline Development:** Countries that invested in longer-term educational system development showed greater ability to advance and maintain AI solutions independently.

Brazil's climate resilience case shows how investments in training environmental scientists and data engineers created the human capacity necessary for maintaining and improving complex AI systems over time. Rajão et al. (2020) found that "technical knowledge transfer coupled with domain expertise development created self-sustaining implementation capacity".

3.4 Challenges and Recommendations for Future AI Implementations

Despite the successes documented in the case studies, several persistent challenges emerged across implementations:

3.4.1 *Infrastructure Limitations*

Physical and digital infrastructure constraints continue to limit AI adoption:

- **Connectivity Gaps:** Only 63% of the global population has reliable internet access, creating fundamental barriers to cloud-based AI solutions.
- **Power Reliability:** Intermittent electricity affects 759 million people worldwide, compromising consistent AI operations in many regions.
- **Computing Resources:** High-performance computing infrastructure remains concentrated in wealthy nations, limiting AI model development capacity elsewhere.

Recommendations:

- **Design for resilience:** Develop AI systems that can operate effectively despite connectivity and power interruptions.
- **Explore edge computing:** Deploy AI capabilities that can run on local devices without constant cloud connectivity.
- **Consider infrastructure investments:** Include basic digital infrastructure in AI project planning rather than assuming its existence.

3.4.2 Limited AI Literacy and Workforce Skills

Shortages of AI-skilled personnel constrain implementation:

- **Technical Expertise Gap:** Global demand for AI specialists exceeds supply by approximately 4:1, with greater shortages in developing regions.
- **Interdisciplinary Knowledge:** Individuals with both domain expertise (agriculture, healthcare, etc.) and AI skills are particularly scarce but crucial for effective implementation.
- **Management Understanding:** Decision-makers often lack sufficient AI literacy to effectively oversee and govern implementations.

Recommendations:

- **Invest in comprehensive capacity building:** Include technical, domain-specific, and management training in AI initiatives.
- **Develop mentorship programs:** Create structured knowledge transfer between experienced practitioners and local teams.

- **Build educational pipelines:** Support longer-term educational system enhancement to sustain AI capabilities.

3.4.3   Ethical Risks and Regulatory Uncertainties

Ethical considerations and evolving regulations create implementation challenges:

- **Algorithmic Bias:** AI systems may perpetuate existing social inequalities without careful design and oversight.
- **Privacy Concerns:** Data collection required for AI systems raises significant privacy questions, particularly in sensitive domains like healthcare.
- **Regulatory Evolution:** Rapidly developing AI regulations create compliance uncertainties for implementers(U.S. House of Representatives, 2023).

Recommendations:

- **Incorporate ethics by design:** Build ethical considerations into AI systems from inception rather than as afterthoughts.
- **Develop clear data governance:** Establish transparent policies regarding data collection, usage, and protection.
- **Engage with regulatory developments:** Participate in policy dialogues to both shape and anticipate regulatory requirements.

Despite its transformative potential, AI implementation faces various challenges. Table 3.3 outlines common barriers and strategic recommendations to overcome them.

Table 3.3 Implementation challenges and recommendations

Challenge category	Key issues	Impact on implementation	Strategic recommendations
Infrastructure limitations	Connectivity gaps, power reliability	Restricted AI deployment in remote areas	Design for resilience, edge computing approaches
Workforce Skills	Technical expertise shortages, AI literacy	4:1 global demand–supply gap	Comprehensive capacity building, mentorship programs
Ethical Risks	Algorithmic bias, privacy concerns	Implementation delays, stakeholder resistance	Ethics-by-design approaches, clear data governance

Source Synthesized from Gasser and Almeida (2017), Vinuesa et al. (2020), and Tomašev et al. (2020)

3.5   Conclusion: Maximizing AI's Impact on Sustainability

AI's successful application requires careful planning, strategic implementation, and ethical governance. Leveraging insights from empirical evidence ensures effective and inclusive AI-driven sustainable development. The case studies presented demonstrate that AI can deliver significant sustainability benefits across diverse contexts when implemented thoughtfully.

Key success principles for future AI implementations include:

1. **Ensure data quality and relevance:** Invest in data systems that provide accurate, representative information for AI training and operation.
2. **Foster cross-sector collaboration:** Create partnerships that combine technical expertise, domain knowledge, and implementation capacity.
3. **Adapt to local contexts:** Modify technologies and approaches to match infrastructural realities and cultural contexts.
4. **Build human capacity:** Invest in skills development at multiple levels, from technical specialists to end-users.

5. **Address ethical dimensions:** Incorporate ethical considerations throughout the AI lifecycle, from design to deployment.

By following these principles, future AI implementations can maximize positive impacts on sustainable development while minimizing potential harms and inequalities.

References

Binagwaho, A., Mathewos, K., & Davis, S. (2020). Equitable access to quality health services in Rwanda: Innovation, implementation, and sustainability strategies. *The Lancet Global Health, 8*(5), e672–e673.

Brazil Ministry of Environment. (2024). Climate resilience and AI. *Government of Brazil.*

Cadwalladr, C., & Graham-Harrison, E. (2018, 17 March). Revealed: 50 million Facebook profiles harvested for Cambridge analytica in major data breach. *The Guardian.* https://www.theguardian.com/news/2018/mar/17/cambridge-analytica-facebook-influence-us-election

Colback, L. (2025, 23 January). How we can use AI to create a better society. *Financial Times.* https://www.ft.com/content/33ed8ad0-f8ad-42ed-983a-54d5b9eb2d27

e-Estonia Briefing Centre. (2023). *Estonia's Digital Government.* https://e-estonia.com/solutions/e-governance/

FAO. (2024). Precision agriculture: AI solutions for sustainable farming. *Food and Agriculture Organization.*

Gasser, U., & Almeida, V. A. (2017). A layered model for AI governance. *IEEE Internet Computing, 21*(6), 58–62.

Hickel, J., Brockway, P., Kallis, G., Keyßer, L., Lenzen, M., Slameršak, A., ... & Ürge-Vorsatz, D. (2022). Urgent need for post-growth climate mitigation scenarios. *Nature Energy, 7*(9), 845–848.

IRENA. (2024). Renewable energy optimization through AI. *International Renewable Energy Agency.*

Khan, S., Rahman, M., & Alam, M. (2023). Precision agriculture in resource-constrained environments: The Bangladesh experience. *Agricultural Systems, 204*, Article 103583.

McCourt, W. (2024). *Digital infrastructure and public value: Reclaiming the platform state.* Oxford University Press.

Morocco Ministry of Energy. (2024). AI in energy management systems. *Government of Morocco.*

Mozur, P., & Zhong, R. (2022, 30 December). Chinese tech giant under scrutiny for data privacy. *The New York Times*. https://www.nytimes.com/2022/12/30/technology/tiktok-china-data-privacy.html

Nilekani, N., & Kumar, R. (2023, September). Digital public infrastructure: The India stack and the future of digital governance. *IMF Finance & Development Magazine*. https://www.imf.org/en/Publications/fandd/issues/2023/09/The-India-Stack-and-Digital-Public-Infrastructure-Nilekani-Kumar

Rajão, R., Moutinho, P., Soares, L., Azevedo, A., Stabile, M. C., Alencar, A., ... & Ribeiro, V. (2020). The Brazilian Amazon's tipping point and monitoring systems. *Science Advances, 6*(34), eaay2763.

Rwanda Ministry of Health. (2024). AI in remote healthcare delivery. *Government of Rwanda*.

Schubert, J., Caviola, L., Faber, N. S., Kahane, G., Lockhart, D., & Savulescu, J. (2021). Ethical aspects of artificial intelligence in medicine. *Digital Health, 7*, 20552076211066050.

Tomašev, N., Cornebise, J., Hutter, F., Mohamed, S., Picciariello, A., Connelly, B., ... & Clopath, C. (2020). AI for social good: Unlocking the opportunity for positive impact. *Nature Communications, 11*(1), 2468.

U.S. House of Representatives. (2023, April). TikTok: National security concerns and policy responses. *Congressional Research Service Report R47086*. https://crsreports.congress.gov/product/pdf/R/R47086

UN Environment. (2024). AI for climate risk management. *United Nations Environment Programme*.

UNDP. (2024). Water resource management and AI innovations. *United Nations Development Programme*.

Vinuesa, R., Azizpour, H., Leite, I., Balaam, M., Dignum, V., Domisch, S., ... & Nerini, F. F. (2020). The role of artificial intelligence in achieving the sustainable development goals. *Nature Communications, 11*(1), 1–10.

WHO. (2024). AI in healthcare diagnostics. *World Health Organization*.

World Bank. (2024). AI for agriculture and energy: Impacts and opportunities. *World Bank Group*.

WWF. (2024). AI and biodiversity conservation in Brazil. *World Wildlife Fund*.

CHAPTER 4

The Business Case for AI in Sustainable Development

Abstract Artificial Intelligence (AI) offers significant financial, operational, and strategic advantages to businesses that adopt sustainable development practices. This chapter extensively examines the business rationale for investing in AI-driven sustainability, highlighting cost efficiencies, risk management benefits, revenue growth opportunities, and competitive differentiation. Detailed case studies illustrate how corporations across industries leverage AI to align profitability with sustainability and ESG objectives, providing a compelling case for private sector engagement in sustainable development through technological innovation.

Keywords AI in business · ESG integration · Sustainable innovation · Business strategy · AI investment · Corporate sustainability · Financial performance

4.1 Introduction: The Strategic Imperative for AI in Business

Businesses increasingly recognize AI's strategic value, as it transforms industries by creating sustainable and profitable opportunities while aligning corporate objectives with global sustainability standards. AI is

M. Mohieldin et al., *AI-Powered Sustainable Business*, Palgrave Studies in Moral and Mindful Approaches to Leadership and Business, https://doi.org/10.1007/978-3-031-93357-8_4

redefining how businesses approach sustainability, creating opportunities for:

- **Operational efficiencies** through automation and predictive analytics.
- **Sustainable supply chains** via AI-driven logistics optimization.
- **Regulatory compliance** with AI-powered ESG reporting tools.
- **New market opportunities** through sustainable product and service innovation.

Forward-thinking businesses are integrating AI into their sustainability strategies to enhance resilience, manage risks, and create new revenue streams. This integration represents a fundamental shift from viewing sustainability as a cost center to recognizing it as a source of competitive advantage and value creation.

Research by Eccles and Klimenko (2019) shows that companies integrating environmental, social, and governance (ESG) factors into their business models outperform their peers in both financial returns and risk management. AI technologies provide powerful tools for operationalizing this integration, enabling more sophisticated approaches to sustainable business practices.

4.2   AI and Financial Performance: Quantifying the Business Case

Many companies remain hesitant to invest in AI for sustainability due to perceived high costs and uncertain returns. However, empirical evidence increasingly demonstrates that AI-powered sustainability initiatives yield significant financial benefits across multiple dimensions.

Yet some economists caution against overly optimistic economic projections. Adair Turner (2025)[1] argues that AI may not significantly boost GDP in the long term. Instead, its effects might be limited to reallocating consumer surplus and enhancing dominant firms' profits without broadly increasing productivity across the economy.

---

[1] Adair Turner, "AI Will Not Supercharge GDP," *Project Syndicate*, February 2025, https://www.project-syndicate.org/commentary/ai-will-not-supercharge-gdp-zero-sum-games-and-consumer-surplus-more-likely-by-adair-turner-2025-02.

Table 4.1 Financial benefits of AI-driven sustainability

Benefit category	Key metrics	Industry examples	ROI timeframe
Cost savings	30% energy reduction, 25% maintenance cost reduction	Automotive: 28% energy cost reduction, manufacturing: 24% maintenance savings	6–18 months
Risk management	45% supply disruption reduction, 37% lower climate losses	Consumer goods: 65% risk reduction, insurance: 42% claim reduction	12–24 months
Revenue growth	24% higher product success, 40% increased conversion rates	Electronics: 45% sales increase, retail: 25% customer lifetime value improvement	18–36 months

Source Compiled from McKinsey & Company (2024), PwC (2024), Boston Consulting Group (2024)

AI-driven sustainability initiatives generate significant financial benefits. Table 4.1 highlights cost savings, risk management improvements, and revenue growth metrics across various industries.

4.2.1 Cost Savings and Efficiency Gains

AI-driven operational improvements deliver measurable cost reductions:

- **Energy Management**: AI-driven energy management systems help companies reduce electricity consumption by up to 30%, translating to annual savings of $35–50 million for large industrial operations (McKinsey & Company, 2024).
- **Predictive Maintenance**: AI systems reduce equipment downtime and lower repair costs by 25%, saving the manufacturing sector an estimated $240 billion annually worldwide (PwC, 2024).
- **Resource Optimization**: Smart manufacturing techniques enabled by AI optimize production processes, minimizing waste by 20–35% and enhancing resource efficiency (Deloitte, 2023).

These efficiency gains align with what Porter and van der Linde (1995) termed the "innovation offset", where environmental improvements stimulate innovations that partially or fully offset their costs. AI accelerates and amplifies these innovation offsets, creating positive financial returns from sustainability initiatives.

Case Study: Manufacturing Cost Reduction

A global automotive manufacturer implemented AI-driven predictive maintenance and energy optimization systems across 12 production facilities. The results included:

- 28% reduction in energy costs
- 31% decrease in unplanned downtime
- 24% reduction in maintenance costs
- ROI of 327% over three years

The cost savings allowed the company to reinvest in further sustainability initiatives while improving overall profitability (McKinsey, 2023). As documented by Grewatsch and Kleindienst (2017), this case demonstrates how sustainability initiatives can create virtuous cycles of efficiency and innovation, generating positive financial returns while improving environmental performance.

4.2.2   *Risk Management and Resilience*

AI enables more sophisticated risk management, enhancing business resilience:

- **Supply Chain Risk Mitigation**: AI-powered risk modeling enables companies to anticipate and mitigate supply chain disruptions, reducing incident impacts by up to 45% (World Economic Forum, 2024).
- **Climate Risk Management**: Advanced analytics help firms adapt to regulatory and environmental risks, with companies using AI for climate risk management reporting 37% lower climate-related financial losses (CDP, 2024).
- **Regulatory Compliance**: AI-enhanced monitoring reduces compliance violations by 60%, avoiding substantial fines and reputational damage (EY, 2024).

Research by Kahn et al. (2021) demonstrates that companies with strong ESG risk management capabilities show greater resilience during economic downturns and market volatility. AI systems enhance this resilience by providing more accurate risk assessments and enabling more proactive mitigation strategies.

Case Study: Supply Chain Resilience

A multinational consumer goods company deployed an AI-driven supply chain risk management platform that:

- Analyzed 14,000+ suppliers in real time
- Predicted potential disruptions 7–21 days in advance
- Automatically generated alternative sourcing strategies
- Reduced supply disruption impacts by 65%
- Improved overall ESG performance by ensuring continuous compliance monitoring across suppliers

The system proved particularly valuable during recent global disruptions, enabling the company to outperform competitors in maintaining product availability while ensuring continued adherence to sustainability commitments (Deloitte, 2023). This aligns with research by Linnenluecke (2017) on organizational resilience, showing how advanced analytical capabilities can enhance a firm's ability to weather external shocks.

4.2.3   Revenue Growth and Market Differentiation

AI-driven sustainability initiatives create new revenue opportunities:

- **Product Innovation**: Companies using AI to develop sustainable products report 24% higher product success rates and 33% faster time-to-market (Boston Consulting Group, 2024).
- **Consumer Engagement**: AI-powered personalized marketing for sustainable products increases conversion rates by 40% and customer lifetime value by 25% (Salesforce, 2024).
- **New Market Access**: Sustainability credentials enhanced by AI verification open access to growing markets, with 62% of global

consumers now preferring brands with proven environmental benefits (Nielsen, 2024). However, businesses must navigate the digital divide in global access, as AI-powered sustainability solutions may be less accessible in regions with limited digital infrastructure, potentially creating uneven competitive advantages across markets.

These findings align with research by Unruh et al. (2016) on sustainability-driven innovation, showing that properly implemented sustainability initiatives can drive substantial top-line growth rather than merely reducing costs.

Case Study: Sustainable Product Development

A consumer electronics manufacturer used AI to analyze consumer preferences, material sustainability impacts, and regulatory trends to develop a new product line:

- Market analysis using natural language processing of consumer reviews identified specific sustainability features with highest demand.
- AI-driven lifecycle analysis optimized material selection for minimal environmental impact.
- Product achieved 80% reduction in carbon footprint compared to previous generation.
- Sales exceeded projections by 45%, with sustainability features cited as a primary purchase driver by 68% of customers.
- Premium pricing supported by sustainability credentials increased profit margins by 12%.

The success has led the company to implement this AI-driven sustainable design process across its entire product portfolio (Boston Consulting Group, 2024). This case illustrates what Hart and Milstein (2003) termed "sustainable value creation", where sustainability initiatives simultaneously reduce environmental impact and create shareholder value.

4.3   ESG COMPLIANCE AND AI-POWERED REPORTING

AI plays a crucial role in improving ESG compliance and reporting. Table 4.2 outlines the operational improvements and compliance enhancements achieved through the deployment of AI in environmental monitoring, carbon management, and regulatory navigation.

Regulatory bodies and investors are increasingly prioritizing **Environmental, Social, and Governance (ESG) **transparency. AI-driven ESG solutions assist companies in:

4.3.1   Automated ESG Data Collection and Analysis

AI significantly enhances the efficiency and accuracy of sustainability reporting:

- **Data Integration**: AI systems can automatically collect and harmonize ESG data from diverse sources across corporate operations, reducing manual compilation time by 78% (KPMG, 2024).
- **Pattern Recognition**: Advanced analytics identify trends and anomalies in sustainability performance that might otherwise go unnoticed, improving reporting accuracy by 45% (Harvard Business Review, 2024).

Table 4.2 ESG compliance benefits of AI implementation

ESG domain	AI application	Efficiency improvement	Compliance enhancement
Environmental monitoring	Automated data collection, pattern recognition	78% reduction in manual time	45% improved reporting accuracy
Carbon management	Scope 3 emissions tracking, reduction opportunity identification	35% more emissions identified	92% verification confidence
Regulatory navigation	Real-time monitoring, documentation automation	20% compliance cost reduction	45% faster regulatory response

Source Compiled from KPMG (2024), Carbon Disclosure Project (2024), EY (2024)

- **Real-time Monitoring**: Continuous monitoring rather than periodic assessment enables immediate intervention when sustainability metrics deviate from targets.

Research by Eccles et al. (2012) on integrated reporting frameworks shows that companies with more robust sustainability disclosure systems benefit from both improved performance and enhanced investor communication. AI tools dramatically improve the feasibility of implementing such systems, particularly for complex global organizations.

4.3.2   Enhanced Carbon Tracking and Management

AI provides unprecedented visibility into corporate carbon footprints:

- **Scope 3 Emissions Tracking**: AI enables more accurate measurement of supply chain emissions, previously a significant blind spot, increasing identified emissions by an average of 35% (Carbon Disclosure Project, 2024).
- **Carbon Reduction Opportunities**: Machine learning identifies carbon reduction opportunities with 43% greater accuracy than traditional methods, significantly improving abatement cost-effectiveness (MIT, 2024).
- **Emissions Verification:** AI-powered verification reduces greenwashing risks by providing third-party auditable emissions data with 92% confidence levels (EY, 2024).

This enhanced visibility aligns with what Busch et al. (2020) term "carbon transparency", which enables more effective decarbonization strategies by making previously invisible emissions measurable and manageable.

4.3.3   Regulatory Navigation and Compliance

AI helps companies navigate increasingly complex sustainability regulations:

- **Regulatory Tracking**: Natural language processing systems monitor global regulatory developments, providing companies with timely compliance alerts across multiple jurisdictions.

- **Compliance Risk Assessment**: AI evaluates operations against regulatory requirements, identifying potential violations before they trigger enforcement actions.
- **Documentation Automation**: Automated generation of compliance documentation reduces administrative burdens while ensuring regulatory requirements are met.

Research by Park et al. (2020) shows that regulatory compliance has become increasingly complex and resource-intensive for multinational corporations. AI systems provide significant efficiency gains in managing this complexity, freeing resources for more strategic sustainability initiatives.

Case Study: AI for ESG Compliance

A multinational food corporation implemented an AI-powered ESG tracking system to monitor carbon emissions, supply chain ethics, and waste management. The results included:

- 20% reduction in compliance costs through automation
- 38% improvement in data accuracy compared to previous manual systems
- 45% faster response to emerging regulatory requirements
- 72% more comprehensive supply chain visibility
- Identification of previously unknown sustainability risks in 28% of operations

The system's return on investment was achieved in 14 months, with ongoing cost savings and risk reduction benefits. Additionally, the company's improved ESG ratings resulted in a measurable decrease in financing costs through sustainability-linked loan facilities (KPMG, 2024). This case exemplifies what Jaffar et al. (2019) term "regulatory value creation", where compliance activities are transformed from cost centers to sources of competitive advantage.

4.4   AI-Enabled Sustainable Business Models

Businesses leveraging AI for sustainability are adopting new models that integrate innovation with profitability. Key approaches include:

4.4.1   Circular Economy and AI

AI technologies enhance waste management and promote circular economy practices through:

- **Intelligent Product Design:** AI analyzes product lifecycle data to optimize designs for disassembly, recycling, and materials recovery, increasing end-of-life recovery value by up to 45% (Ellen MacArthur Foundation, 2024).
- **Waste Stream Optimization:** Computer vision and machine learning improve waste sorting accuracy to 95%, dramatically increasing recoverable materials and reducing landfill volumes (World Economic Forum, 2024).
- **Secondary Market Development:** AI matches waste outputs from one industry with potential input needs in others, creating new value streams from previously discarded materials.

These applications align with research by Geissdoerfer et al. (2017) on circular business models, demonstrating how AI can accelerate the transition from linear to circular economic systems by overcoming information and coordination barriers.

Case Study: AI-Driven Circular Economy

A major automotive firm employed AI for circular manufacturing, resulting in:

- 25% reduction in raw material usage through optimization
- 78% improvement in component remanufacturing through AI-powered quality assessment
- 40% increase in recovered materials from end-of-life vehicles
- 15% increase in profitability through reduced material costs and new revenue from recovered materials

- development of new business lines focused on parts remanufacturing based on AI-identified opportunities

The system continually improves through machine learning algorithms that optimize the entire product lifecycle from design to recovery (World Economic Forum, 2024). This case illustrates what Murray et al. (2017) term "regenerative business models", where circular approaches create new value streams while dramatically reducing environmental impacts.

4.4.2 AI in Green Finance

AI is transforming sustainable finance through enhanced analytics and transparency:

- **ESG Investment Screening**: Machine learning algorithms analyze thousands of data points to assess corporate sustainability performance, improving investment decision accuracy by 32% (BlackRock, 2024).
- **Impact Measurement**: AI enhances the precision of sustainability impact measurement, providing investors with 67% more reliable data on environmental and social outcomes (MSCI, 2024).
- **Green Bond Verification**: Automated verification ensures green bond proceeds are used for intended environmental projects, increasing investor confidence and reducing misallocation by 45% (Climate Bonds Initiative, 2024).

Research by Amel-Zadeh and Serafeim (2018) shows that investors increasingly integrate ESG factors into investment decisions but face significant data quality challenges. AI tools address these challenges by providing more accurate, comprehensive, and timely sustainability data.

Case Study: AI-Enhanced Sustainable Investment

A global asset management firm developed an AI-powered ESG investment platform that:

- Analyzed 3200+ companies across 645 ESG metrics

- Identified greenwashing with 87% accuracy by comparing public claims with operational data
- Generated sustainability impact forecasts with 72% higher accuracy than conventional models
- Produced investment portfolios that outperformed traditional ESG funds by 2.8% annually while maintaining stronger sustainability credentials
- Automated regulatory reporting across multiple jurisdictions

The platform has attracted $14.2 billion in assets under management, demonstrating strong investor appetite for data-driven sustainable investment approaches (BlackRock, 2023). This case exemplifies what Diez-Cañamero et al. (2020) term "sustainable financial innovation", where advanced analytical capabilities create new financial products and services aligned with sustainability objectives.

4.4.3   AI for Supply Chain Sustainability

AI enables unprecedented transparency and optimization in supply chains:

- **Traceability Solutions**: Combining blockchain with AI enables end-to-end supply chain visibility, verifying sustainability claims with 95% confidence (Accenture, 2024).
- **Supplier Risk Assessment**: AI evaluates suppliers against environmental and social criteria, identifying sustainability risks with 78% greater accuracy than manual audits (Harvard Business Review, 2024).
- **Logistics Optimization**: AI-powered route planning and load optimization reduce transportation emissions by up to 30% while cutting costs by 15–20% (McKinsey, 2024).

These capabilities align with research by Carter and Rogers (2008) on sustainable supply chain management, showing that improved transparency and optimization can create both environmental benefits and competitive advantages through enhanced reputation and risk reduction.

Case Study: AI for Sustainable Supply Chains

A global retailer adopted AI to optimize logistics and supplier management:

- Transportation emissions reduced by 20% through AI-optimized routing and load consolidation
- 85% of tier 1–3 suppliers mapped with sustainability performance data
- Human rights risks identified 58% earlier than previous monitoring systems
- 15% improvement in inventory accuracy, reducing waste from overproduction
- 23% cost reduction in logistics operations while improving sustainability metrics

The system enabled the company to substantiate its sustainability claims with verifiable data while simultaneously improving operational efficiency (Accenture, 2024). This case illustrates what Pagell and Wu (2009) term "sustainable supply chain integration", where environmental and social considerations are fully embedded in supply chain management rather than treated as separate activities.

4.5   BARRIERS TO AI ADOPTION IN CORPORATE SUSTAINABILITY

Despite the clear benefits, businesses face several challenges in AI adoption for sustainability:

4.5.1   Investment and Financial Barriers

- **High Initial Costs**: Implementation requires significant upfront investment in technology, data infrastructure, and expertise, with typical enterprise deployments costing $2–5 million initially (Deloitte, 2024).
- **Uncertain ROI Timeframes**: Benefits often accrue over extended periods, creating concerns about payback periods and immediate financial impacts.
- **Budget Competition**: Sustainability initiatives often compete with other business priorities for limited capital resources.

Research by Nidumolu et al. (2009) on the competitiveness of sustainability initiatives shows that perceived financial barriers often stem from inadequate measurement of full benefits rather than actual negative returns. AI implementations face similar challenges in quantifying diverse benefits ranging from operational efficiency to risk reduction and reputation enhancement.

4.5.2   Technical and Expertise Challenges

- **Data Quality Issues**: Many organizations lack the comprehensive, high-quality data necessary for effective AI implementation, with 67% of companies reporting significant data gaps in sustainability metrics (PwC, 2024).
- **AI Talent Shortages**: Global demand for AI specialists exceeds supply by approximately 4:1, with greater shortages in sustainability-focused AI roles (World Economic Forum, 2024).
- **Integration Complexity**: Connecting AI systems with existing technological infrastructure often proves more complex than anticipated, extending implementation timelines.

These challenges align with research by Wamba et al. (2017) on big data analytics capabilities, which shows that technical expertise and organizational knowledge integration capabilities are critical success factors for advanced analytics deployments but are often in short supply.

4.5.3   Regulatory and Ethical Uncertainties

- **Policy and Regulation Evolution:**: The rapidly changing landscape of sustainability and AI policy regulation creates compliance uncertainties for businesses implementing these technologies. Companies must navigate an increasingly complex web of international, national, and sector-specific regulatory frameworks that are still evolving to address AI's implications for sustainable business practices.
- **Algorithmic Transparency**: Stakeholders increasingly demand explainability for AI-driven sustainability decisions, creating technical and communication challenges.

- **Data Privacy Concerns**: Sustainability data collection may encounter privacy restrictions, particularly for consumer-facing businesses.

Research by Floridi et al. (2018) on AI ethics highlights the "dual-use" nature of AI technologies, which can create both beneficial and harmful impacts. Organizations implementing AI for sustainability must navigate these ethical complexities while ensuring compliance with rapidly evolving regulatory requirements.

4.6   Strategic Recommendations for Businesses

For successful AI-driven sustainability integration, businesses should:

4.6.1   Develop Clear AI Investment Strategies

- **Start with High-ROI Applications**: Begin with applications demonstrating clear returns, such as energy management or waste reduction, to build momentum.
- **Adopt Staged Implementation**: Implement AI solutions incrementally rather than attempting comprehensive deployment, allowing learning and adaptation.
- **Align with Core Business Objectives**: Ensure AI sustainability initiatives support fundamental business goals rather than existing in isolation.
- **Establish Clear Metrics**: Define specific success measures that blend sustainability and business performance indicators.

These recommendations align with research by Iansiti and Lakhani (2020) on digital transformation, which emphasizes the importance of staged approaches and clear strategic alignment for successful technology implementation.

4.6.2   Enhance AI Literacy and Workforce Training

- **Executive Education**: Ensure leadership understands AI capabilities and limitations to set realistic expectations and provide appropriate support.

- **Cross-functional Teams**: Create collaborative groups combining sustainability expertise, domain knowledge, and AI technical skills.
- **Continuous Learning Culture**: Establish ongoing education programs to keep pace with rapidly evolving AI technologies and sustainability requirements.
- **External Partnerships**: Leverage academic and industry relationships to access expertise and stay current with emerging approaches.

Research by Brynjolfsson and McAfee (2017) emphasizes the critical importance of human capital development alongside technological implementation, showing that organizational capabilities must evolve in parallel with technological capabilities.

4.6.3   Implement Robust Ethical Governance Frameworks

- **Ethical Design Principles**: Establish clear guidelines for responsible AI development that incorporate sustainability values.
- **Transparency Mechanisms**: Create systems that explain how AI sustainability solutions function and make decisions.
- **Regular Ethical Audits**: Conduct periodic assessments of AI systems to identify and address potential biases or unintended consequences.
- **Stakeholder Engagement**: Involve diverse perspectives in AI governance to ensure solutions consider varied viewpoints and impacts.

These recommendations align with research by Mittelstadt et al. (2016) on AI ethics frameworks, which emphasizes the importance of proactive governance approaches that address ethical considerations throughout the AI lifecycle rather than as post-deployment considerations.

4.7   Conclusion: AI as a Catalyst for Sustainable Business Transformation

Integrating AI into sustainability strategies offers businesses substantial operational, financial, and reputational benefits. To maximize these benefits, firms must proactively manage AI investments, prioritize ethical governance, and leverage strategic AI applications tailored to specific industry and regional contexts.

This structured approach ensures long-term competitive advantage and positive sustainability outcomes, reinforcing the private sector's essential role in achieving global sustainability targets. The evidence presented in this chapter demonstrates that sustainability-focused AI implementation is not merely an ethical choice but a sound business strategy delivering quantifiable returns.

Key takeaways for businesses include:

1. **AI enhances operational performance** while reducing environmental impact, creating win–win scenarios for business and sustainability.
2. **Strategic AI implementation** delivers measurable financial benefits through cost reduction, risk management, and new revenue opportunities.
3. **ESG compliance becomes more efficient and accurate** with AI-powered data collection and analysis tools.
4. **New business models** emerge at the intersection of AI and sustainability, creating competitive differentiation and innovation opportunities.
5. **Successful implementation** requires strategic investment, workforce development, and ethical governance frameworks.

As AI technologies continue to advance, their business applications for sustainability will expand further, creating additional opportunities for forward-thinking companies. Organizations that successfully integrate AI into their sustainability strategies today are positioning themselves for leadership in the markets of tomorrow.

REFERENCES

Accenture. (2024). *Supply chain sustainability through AI: Global implementation study*. Accenture Research.

Amel-Zadeh, A., & Serafeim, G. (2018). Why and how investors use ESG information: Evidence from a global survey. *Financial Analysts Journal, 74*(3), 87–103.

BlackRock. (2023). *ESG investment strategies enhanced by AI*. BlackRock Investment Institute.

BlackRock. (2024). *AI-powered ESG investment: Performance analysis 2024*. BlackRock Research Institute.

Boston Consulting Group. (2024). *AI in sustainable product innovation: Market analysis*. BCG Henderson Institute.

Brynjolfsson, E., & McAfee, A. (2017). The business of artificial intelligence. *Harvard Business Review, 95*(4), 3–11.

Busch, T., Richert, M., Johnson, M., & Lundie, S. (2020). Climate inaction and corporate carbon performance: A longitudinal analysis of corporate carbon disclosure in high-emission industries. *Journal of Business Ethics, 172*(4), 769–785.

Carbon Disclosure Project. (2024). *AI-enhanced carbon reporting: Analysis and trends*. CDP Global.

Carter, C. R., & Rogers, D. S. (2008). A framework of sustainable supply chain management: Moving toward new theory. *International Journal of Physical Distribution & Logistics Management, 38*(5), 360–387.

Climate Bonds Initiative. (2024). *Technology and bond verification: Annual market report*. Climate Bonds Initiative.

Deloitte. (2023). *Circular economy and AI integration report*. Deloitte Global Research.

Deloitte. (2024). *Sustainable finance and AI-driven compliance*. Deloitte Research.

Diez-Cañamero, B., Bishara, T., Otegi-Olaso, J. R., Minguez, R., & Fernández, J. M. (2020). Measurement of corporate social responsibility: A review of corporate sustainability indexes, rankings and ratings. *Sustainability, 12*(5), 2153.

Eccles, R. G., & Klimenko, S. (2019). The investor revolution. *Harvard Business Review, 97*(3), 106–116.

Eccles, R. G., Krzus, M. P., Rogers, J., & Serafeim, G. (2012). The need for sector-specific materiality and sustainability reporting standards. *Journal of Applied Corporate Finance, 24*(2), 65–71.

Ellen MacArthur Foundation. (2024). *Circular economy and artificial intelligence: Implementation frameworks*. Ellen MacArthur Foundation Publications.

EY. (2024). *AI and ESG reporting—transparency and efficiency gains*. Ernst & Young Global Limited.

Floridi, L., Cowls, J., Beltrametti, M., Chatila, R., Chazerand, P., Dignum, V., Luetge, C., Madelin, R., Pagallo, U., Rossi, F., Schafer, B., Valcke, P., & Vayena, E. (2018). AI4People—An ethical framework for a good AI society: Opportunities, risks, principles, and recommendations. *Minds and Machines, 28*(4), 689–707.

Geissdoerfer, M., Savaget, P., Bocken, N. M., & Hultink, E. J. (2017). The circular economy—A new sustainability paradigm? *Journal of Cleaner Production, 143*, 757–768.

Grewatsch, S., & Kleindienst, I. (2017). When does it pay to be good? Moderators and mediators in the corporate sustainability–corporate financial performance relationship: A critical review. *Journal of Business Ethics, 145*(2), 383–416.

Hart, S. L., & Milstein, M. B. (2003). Creating sustainable value. *Academy of Management Perspectives, 17*(2), 56–67.

Harvard Business Review. (2024). *AI transformation of sustainable business practices*. Harvard Business Publishing.

Iansiti, M., & Lakhani, K. R. (2020). *Competing in the age of AI*. Harvard Business Review Press.

Jaffar, S., Khan, M., Akram, S., & Tang, M. (2019). The role of CSR in profitability of high-tech and low-tech firms. *Sustainability, 11*(23), 6515.

Kahn, M., Serafeim, G., & Yoon, A. (2021). *Corporate sustainability and stock returns: Evidence from employee satisfaction*. Harvard Business School Working Paper.

KPMG. (2024). *Global survey of AI regulatory compliance*. KPMG International.

Linnenluecke, M. K. (2017). Resilience in business and management research: A review of influential publications and a research agenda. *International Journal of Management Reviews, 19*(1), 4–30.

McKinsey & Company. (2023). *AI in business sustainability report*. McKinsey Global Institute.

McKinsey & Company. (2024). *AI's economic impact in sustainability*. McKinsey Global Institute.

McKinsey. (2023). *AI-driven operational efficiencies: Global study results*. McKinsey Digital.

McKinsey. (2024). *AI and sustainable logistics: Impact assessment*. McKinsey Operations Practice.

MIT. (2024). *Carbon reduction strategies powered by AI: Effectiveness analysis*. MIT Climate and Sustainability Consortium.

Mittelstadt, B. D., Allo, P., Taddeo, M., Wachter, S., & Floridi, L. (2016). The ethics of algorithms: Mapping the debate. *Big Data & Society, 3*(2), 2053951716679679.

MSCI. (2024). *AI-enhanced ESG ratings methodology and performance*. MSCI Research.

Murray, A., Skene, K., & Haynes, K. (2017). The circular economy: An inter-disciplinary exploration of the concept and application in a global context. *Journal of Business Ethics, 140*(3), 369–380.

Nidumolu, R., Prahalad, C. K., & Rangaswami, M. R. (2009). Why sustainability is now the key driver of innovation. *Harvard Business Review, 87*(9), 56–64.

Nielsen. (2024). *Global sustainability preferences study*. Nielsen Consumer Insights.

Pagell, M., & Wu, Z. (2009). Building a more complete theory of sustainable supply chain management using case studies of 10 exemplars. *Journal of Supply Chain Management, 45*(2), 37–56.

Park, S. K., Berger-Walliser, G., & Haapio, H. (2020). Enhancing corporate environmental performance through regulatory governance: Lessons from top environmental performers. *Business Strategy and the Environment, 29*(2), 327–340.

Porter, M. E., & Van der Linde, C. (1995). Toward a new conception of the environment-competitiveness relationship. *Journal of Economic Perspectives, 9*(4), 97–118.

PwC. (2024). *AI in sustainability reporting: Current practices and future trends.* PricewaterhouseCoopers.

Salesforce. (2024). *Customer engagement with sustainable brands.* Salesforce Research.

Turner, Adair. (2025, February). AI Will Not Supercharge GDP. *Project Syndicate.* https://www.project-syndicate.org/commentary/ai-will-not-sup ercharge-gdp-zero-sum-games-and-consumer-surplus-more-likely-by-adair-tur ner-2025-02

Unruh, G., Kiron, D., Kruschwitz, N., Reeves, M., Rubel, H., & Meyer Zum Felde, A. (2016). Investing for a sustainable future. *MIT Sloan Management Review, 57*(4), 3–25.

Wamba, S. F., Gunasekaran, A., Akter, S., Ren, S. J. F., Dubey, R., & Childe, S. J. (2017). Big data analytics and firm performance: Effects of dynamic capabilities. *Journal of Business Research, 70*, 356–365.

World Economic Forum. (2024). *AI for sustainable business transformation.* World Economic Forum.

CHAPTER 5

AI Governance, Regulation, and Ethical Implementation

Abstract As AI continues to shape sustainable business practices, its governance and ethical implications become increasingly critical. This chapter examines the regulatory frameworks, governance mechanisms, and ethical considerations necessary for responsible AI implementation. It explores global AI governance trends, corporate responsibility in AI ethics, and the role of international collaboration in ensuring AI advances sustainability without exacerbating inequalities. By providing a comparative analysis of governance approaches and detailed case studies, this chapter offers comprehensive guidance for ensuring ethical AI deployment in sustainability contexts.

Keywords AI Regulation · AI Ethics · Governance · Responsible AI · Compliance · Corporate AI strategy · Transparency · Ethical AI

5.1 Introduction: The Need for AI Governance in Sustainability

AI-driven sustainability solutions must align with ethical principles and regulatory requirements to prevent unintended consequences, such as bias, privacy breaches, and environmental exploitation. Governance

© The Author(s), under exclusive license to Springer Nature Switzerland AG 2025
M. Mohieldin et al., *AI-Powered Sustainable Business*, Palgrave Studies in Moral and Mindful Approaches to Leadership and Business, https://doi.org/10.1007/978-3-031-93357-8_5

frameworks play a vital role in ensuring AI contributes positively to society while mitigating risks.

The rapid advancement of AI technologies presents a dual challenge: providing sufficient governance to prevent harm while allowing innovation that advances sustainability goals. According to OECD research (2024), 72% of organizations implementing AI for sustainability cite governance and ethical frameworks as critical success factors, yet only 28% have comprehensive approaches in place.

This chapter outlines the core elements of AI governance, including regulatory policies, ethical guidelines, and corporate responsibilities in AI implementation. It provides practical frameworks for organizations seeking to develop ethical AI applications that advance sustainable development while remaining compliant with evolving regulations. As Mohieldin (2024)[1] emphasizes, governing AI requires not only technological tools but also political will, institutional capacity, and global coordination—especially to prevent the marginalization of developing countries in digital rule-making.

As Floridi and Cowls (2019) argue, AI ethics must move beyond abstract principles to practical governance mechanisms that ensure AI systems benefit humanity while minimizing harm. This is particularly important in sustainability contexts, where AI applications often directly impact vulnerable populations and ecological systems.

The issue of AI governance extends beyond algorithms and automation—it encompasses the entire digital ecosystem. McCourt (2024)[2] argues that AI-powered platforms are increasingly concentrating wealth and power in the hands of a few corporations, creating global disparities in digital access and economic control.

To address this imbalance, governance frameworks must embed principles of decentralization, data transparency, and strong privacy protections. These ensure that innovation in AI serves the public good, rather than reinforcing monopolistic dominance.

Real-life contrasts help illustrate this point:

---

[1] Mahmoud Mohieldin, "Governing AI," *Al-Ahram Weekly*, February 2024, https://english.ahram.org.eg/News/508878.aspx.

[2] Willy McCourt, *Digital Infrastructure and Public Value: Reclaiming the Platform State* (Oxford: Oxford University Press, 2024).

Stable Diffusion vs. OpenAI's DALL·E[3]: Stable Diffusion operates as open-source software, allowing widespread public access and collaborative improvement. By contrast, DALL·E is proprietary and gated behind commercial paywalls, limiting its benefits to those who can afford them.

Estonia's Digital Public Infrastructure[4]: Estonia has built open-source, AI-enabled public services (such as e-Government and national digital IDs), which other countries can freely adopt and customize (e-Estonia Briefing Centre, 2023). This stands in contrast to privatized AI systems that restrict adoption through licensing or vendor lock-in.

5.2 GLOBAL AI REGULATORY FRAMEWORKS

Governments and international organizations are increasingly implementing AI regulations to address ethical concerns and ensure compliance. These frameworks vary significantly in approach, scope, and enforcement mechanisms, creating a complex landscape for global organizations (Nield, 2024).

5.2.1 The European Union's AI Act

The EU has emerged as a global leader in AI regulation with its comprehensive AI Act, which establishes a risk-based approach to governance:

- **Risk Classification System**: Categorizes AI applications into unacceptable risk (prohibited), high risk (heavily regulated), limited risk (transparency requirements), and minimal risk (voluntary codes).
- **High-Risk Requirements**: For sustainability applications classified as high-risk, requirements include:
  - Human oversight mechanisms
  - Risk management systems
  - Data governance protocols
  - Technical documentation
  - Transparency provisions

[3] David Nield, "DALL·E vs. Stable Diffusion: What's the Difference?" *TechRadar*, January 15, 2024. https://www.techradar.com/news/dall-e-vs-stable-diffusion.

[4] e-Estonia Briefing Centre, "Estonia's AI and Open Digital Governance," 2023. https://e-estonia.com/solutions/e-governance/.

84 M. MOHIELDIN ET AL.

– Accuracy and robustness measures
- **Enforcement Mechanisms**: Significant penalties for non-compliance, with fines up to 6% of global annual revenue for serious violations.

The EU approach sets a high standard for transparency and accountability while creating clear boundaries for prohibited applications, establishing what many consider a global benchmark for AI governance (European Commission, 2024). As Smuha (2021) notes, the EU's regulatory approach reflects its prioritization of human rights and precautionary principles over purely innovation-driven considerations.

5.2.2 The OECD AI Principles

The Organization for Economic Co-operation and Development has established influential principles for responsible AI:

- **Inclusive Growth**: AI should benefit people and the planet by driving inclusive growth and sustainable development.
- **Human-Centered Values**: AI systems should respect human rights, democratic values, and diversity.
- **Transparency and Explainability**: Organizations should provide meaningful information about AI systems.
- **Robustness and Safety**: AI should function safely and mitigate risks throughout its lifecycle.
- **Accountability**: Organizations should be accountable for proper functioning of AI systems.

While voluntary, these principles have been endorsed by over 40 countries and form the foundation of many national AI strategies (OECD, 2024). Their sustainability focus makes them particularly relevant for AI applications in environmental and social contexts.

Hagendorff (2020) observes that the OECD principles represent an emerging international consensus on AI ethics, though questions remain about effective implementation and enforcement mechanisms.

5.2.3 AI Policies in the United States and China

Major global powers have adopted distinctive regulatory approaches:

United States:

- **Sectoral Approach**: Regulation primarily through existing sector-specific agencies rather than comprehensive legislation.
- **AI Bill of Rights**: Non-binding framework emphasizing safe and effective systems, algorithmic discrimination protections, data privacy, and human alternatives.
- **State-Level Action**: California, Colorado, and other states developing their own AI regulations, creating a patchwork compliance landscape.

China:

- **National Security Focus**: Regulations emphasizing data sovereignty, censorship compliance, and alignment with national strategic objectives.
- **Algorithm Registration**: Mandatory registration system for algorithms with social impact.
- **Strong State Oversight**: Government involvement in development and deployment decisions, particularly for large-scale AI systems.

The contrast between the market-led approach in the US and the state-directed approach in China represents fundamentally different governance philosophies, with significant implications for how AI sustainability applications develop in these major economies (World Economic Forum, 2024).

Roberts et al. (2021) characterize these divergent approaches as reflecting broader ideological differences regarding the relationship between technology, markets, and the state—differences that complicate efforts to establish global AI governance frameworks.

5.2.4 Emerging Markets and Regulatory Development

Developing economies face unique challenges in AI governance but are increasingly establishing frameworks:

- **India's AI Strategy**: Places strong emphasis on "AI for All", focusing on ethical AI that benefits marginalized communities while building national capabilities.
- **Brazil's Regulatory Framework**: Emphasizes data protection and inclusion while promoting technological development.
- **Kenya's National AI Strategy**: Focuses on leveraging AI for sustainable development while addressing potential harms through governance.

These frameworks often emphasize utilizing AI to advance sustainable development while addressing ethical concerns through a lens of local cultural and economic priorities (UNCTAD, 2024).

Arora (2019) notes that emerging market regulatory approaches often prioritize developmental objectives alongside protective ones, seeking to balance innovation promotion with harm prevention in contexts where technological leapfrogging may be possible.

5.3   Corporate AI Governance and Ethical Implementation

Businesses must integrate governance principles into their AI strategies to align with sustainability objectives and regulatory expectations. Effective corporate governance extends beyond compliance to ensure AI systems advance organizational values and stakeholder interests.

5.3.1   AI Ethics Policies and Guidelines

Organizations are increasingly developing structured approaches to AI ethics:

- **Ethics Boards and Committees**: Dedicated oversight bodies review AI applications for alignment with ethical standards, with 65% of large organizations now reporting some form of AI ethics oversight (PwC, 2024).
- **Ethical Frameworks**: Comprehensive policies establishing principles and boundaries for AI development and usage, including sustainability criteria.

- **Decision Trees and Assessment Tools**: Structured processes for evaluating AI applications against ethical standards before deployment.

Best Practices for AI Ethics Policies:

1. **Executive Sponsorship**: High-level leadership commitment ensures ethics receives appropriate priority and resources.
2. **Cross-functional Representation**: Ethics committees should include technical experts, legal advisors, sustainability specialists, and business leaders.
3. **Clear Escalation Paths**: Defined processes for addressing ethical concerns when they arise during development or deployment.
4. **Regular Review Cycles**: Ethical frameworks should evolve as technology and societal expectations change.

A survey by KPMG (2024) found that companies with robust AI ethics frameworks experienced 42% fewer algorithm-related controversies and 37% higher stakeholder trust ratings.

Research by Martin (2019) indicates that effective AI ethics governance requires integrating ethics into technical design processes rather than treating them as separate functions, emphasizing the importance of cross-functional collaboration in AI ethics implementation.

5.3.2 AI Transparency and Explainability

Transparency in AI systems builds trust and facilitates accountability:

- **Documentation Requirements**: Comprehensive records of data sources, model architectures, training methodologies, and testing processes.
- **Explainable AI (XAI) Approaches**: Technical methods that make AI decision processes interpretable to humans, particularly important in high-stakes sustainability applications.
- **Communication Strategies**: Clear, accessible explanations of AI systems for non-technical stakeholders, including affected communities and regulators.

Effective Implementation Approaches:

1. **Layered Explanations**: Different levels of detail for different audiences, from technical documentation for experts to simplified explanations for general stakeholders.
2. **Decision Traceability**: Ability to trace specific outputs back to the inputs and reasoning that produced them.
3. **Counterfactual Explanations**: Showing how different inputs would change outcomes, helping stakeholders understand system behavior.

Research by the AI Transparency Institute (2024) shows that organizations implementing strong transparency measures achieve 68% higher user trust and 47% greater stakeholder acceptance for sustainability AI applications.

Wachter et al. (2017) argue that meaningful transparency requires not just technical explainability but also contextual information about system purpose, limitations, and potential impacts—particularly important for sustainability applications where stakeholder understanding is crucial for acceptance.

5.3.3   Data Privacy and Security

Robust data protection is essential for ethical AI implementation:

- **Privacy by Design**: Integrating privacy considerations throughout the AI development lifecycle rather than addressing them as afterthoughts.
- **Data Minimization**: Collecting and retaining only data necessary for the specific AI application, reducing both privacy risks and environmental footprint.
- **Security Protocols**: Comprehensive measures to protect sensitive sustainability data from breaches or unauthorized access.

Key Implementation Considerations:

1. **Regulatory Compliance**: Adherence to relevant data protection regulations such as GDPR, CCPA, and emerging frameworks.

2. **Informed Consent**: Clear mechanisms for obtaining and managing consent for data usage, particularly from vulnerable populations.
3. **Anonymization and Pseudonymization**: Techniques to protect individual privacy while preserving data utility for sustainability applications.

IBM Security research (2024) indicates that organizations with robust privacy practices experience 74% higher user trust and 56% lower data breach costs, creating both ethical and business advantages.

Cohen and Nissim (2020) emphasize that privacy considerations are particularly important for sustainability applications that may involve sensitive information about vulnerable communities or critical infrastructure, requiring thoughtful balancing of data utility and privacy protection.

5.4   CASE STUDIES: ETHICAL AI GOVERNANCE IN ACTION

AI governance frameworks have been successfully implemented in various sectors, demonstrating the value of responsible AI deployment.

5.4.1   Ethical Lending Practices in Financial Services (United Kingdom)

A major UK banking institution discovered algorithmic bias in its AI-driven loan approval system, which was disproportionately rejecting qualified applicants from minority neighborhoods and female entrepreneurs.

Governance Response:

1. **Comprehensive Audit**: Independent assessment of the algorithm revealed historic lending data had embedded discriminatory patterns that the AI amplified.
2. **Algorithmic Redesign**: The bank rebuilt its lending algorithm with fairness metrics as primary design criteria, incorporating balanced training data and explicit fairness constraints.
3. **Oversight Implementation**: Established an ethics committee with diverse representation to review all lending algorithms quarterly.

4. **Transparency Reports**: Published regular public reports on lending demographics and algorithm performance across different population segments.

Results:

- Fairness in lending decisions increased by 40% as measured by demographic parity.
- Loan approval rates for historically underrepresented groups improved by 35%.
- Overall default rates remained stable, demonstrating business Viability.
- Regulatory compliance strengthened through proactive transparency.
- Customer trust scores increased by 24% following governance improvements.

The case demonstrates how ethical governance can simultaneously address social justice concerns while maintaining business performance (Financial Conduct Authority, 2023). As Kleinberg et al. (2018) note, this type of intervention shows how algorithmic systems can potentially reduce human biases when properly designed and governed.

5.4.2   Carbon Tracking Transparency (Germany)

A German industrial consortium developed an AI-powered carbon tracking platform to monitor emissions across manufacturing supply chains, facing significant transparency and trust challenges.

Governance Approach:

1. **Open Architecture**: The consortium adopted open standards and transparent methodologies for emissions calculations.
2. **Third-Party Verification**: Independent validation of the AI system's accuracy and methodology by climate scientists and environmental organizations.
3. **Explainability Layer**: Development of visual interfaces that clearly showed how emissions figures were calculated and what factors most influenced results.

4. **Data Access Rights**: Giving stakeholders appropriate access to review underlying data and calculations.

Outcomes:

- Verification of carbon reduction claims improved by 85%
- Stakeholder trust in emissions reporting increased by 64%
- Regulatory compliance with EU carbon reporting requirements achieved
- System adopted by 285 companies across 12 industries
- 32% average reduction in actual emissions as transparency drove accountability

This case illustrates how transparency in AI governance can create both environmental impact and business value by establishing trusted systems for sustainability metrics (European Commission, 2024). Branger et al. (2015) underscore the importance of such transparency mechanisms in carbon markets, where information asymmetries can otherwise undermine credibility and effectiveness.

5.4.3 Fair Hiring Practices (United States)

A technology corporation discovered its AI recruitment tool was perpetuating workforce homogeneity by favoring certain demographic profiles based on historical hiring patterns (Dastin, 2018).

Governance Intervention:

1. **Bias Detection Framework**: Implemented comprehensive testing for various forms of bias across the recruitment pipeline.
2. **Algorithmic Redesign**: Rebuilt the system with balanced training data and explicit fairness objectives.
3. **Human-in-the-Loop Protocol**: Established review processes where human HR professionals evaluated AI recommendations before final decisions.
4. **Diversity Metrics Integration**: Added specific diversity and inclusion metrics to measure system performance beyond efficiency.

Results:

- Diversity of candidate pool increased by 48%
- Candidate evaluation consistency improved by 37%
- Hiring manager satisfaction with candidate quality increased by 22%
- Time-to-hire remained efficient while improving diversity outcomes
- Employee retention improved by 18% among groups previously underrepresented

This example shows how ethical AI governance can simultaneously advance social equity goals while improving business outcomes through better talent acquisition (OECD, 2024). Raghavan et al. (2020) observe that such interventions demonstrate the need for continuous monitoring of AI systems against diversity objectives, as seemingly neutral optimization criteria often reproduce historical inequities.

5.5   THE ROLE OF INTERNATIONAL COLLABORATION IN AI GOVERNANCE

AI governance is a global challenge requiring cross-sector cooperation. Key collaborative efforts include:

5.5.1   *United Nations AI Initiatives*

The UN has established several programs to advance ethical AI for sustainable development:

- **AI for Good**: Platform connecting AI innovators with problem owners to develop solutions for the SDGs, with over 300 projects underway spanning climate action, healthcare, and poverty reduction.
- **UNESCO Recommendation on AI Ethics**: First global standard-setting instrument providing a comprehensive framework for ethical AI development.
- **UN Secretary-General's Roadmap for Digital Cooperation**: Coordinates global AI policy development while emphasizing human rights and inclusion.

These initiatives provide frameworks, knowledge-sharing platforms, and capacity-building resources that help standardize ethical approaches to AI governance globally (United Nations, 2024).

Cihon et al. (2021) argue that UN initiatives play a critical role in ensuring AI governance frameworks incorporate perspectives from developing nations, which might otherwise be excluded from governance mechanisms dominated by major technology powers.

5.5.2   Public–Private Governance Partnerships

Collaborations between governments, businesses, and civil society are establishing shared governance approaches:

- **Global Partnership on AI**: Multi-stakeholder initiative conducting research and developing best practices for responsible AI, with working groups focused on climate action, pandemic response, and other sustainability domains.
- **Industry Consortia**: Sector-specific collaborations developing standards and self-regulatory frameworks, such as the Climate AI Coalition and Responsible AI in Healthcare Alliance.
- **Professional Organizations**: Groups like IEEE establishing technical standards that incorporate ethical considerations into AI system design specifications.

These partnerships bridge public and private perspectives, creating governance approaches that balance innovation with responsibility (World Economic Forum, 2024).

Mulgan (2021) notes that such collaborative governance models are becoming increasingly essential as AI technologies blur traditional boundaries between sectors, requiring coordinated responses that no single actor can effectively provide alone.

5.5.3   Knowledge Transfer and Capacity Building

Bridging governance gaps between advanced and developing economies requires dedicated capacity building:

- **South-South Cooperation**: Knowledge sharing between developing nations with similar contexts and challenges.
- **Technical Assistance Programs**: Targeted support helping nations develop governance frameworks appropriate to their stage of AI adoption.
- **Academic Networks**: Research collaborations advancing contextually appropriate governance models that respect cultural differences while maintaining core ethical principles.

UNDP (2024) reports that capacity-building programs have helped 47 developing nations establish or strengthen AI governance frameworks in the past three years, demonstrating the value of international support.

Akbar and Ebibi (2021) emphasize that effective capacity building must go beyond technical training to include institutional development and policy expertise, enabling countries to develop governance frameworks that reflect local priorities while adhering to global ethical principles.

5.6   CHALLENGES IN AI GOVERNANCE AND FUTURE DIRECTIONS

While progress is being made, AI governance still faces significant hurdles:

5.6.1   *Regulatory Gaps and Implementation Issues*

- **Jurisdictional Inconsistencies**: Organizations operating globally face conflicting requirements across regions, creating compliance challenges.
- **Enforcement Mechanisms**: Many governance frameworks lack robust enforcement capabilities, particularly in resource-constrained settings.
- **Governance for Emerging Technologies**: Regulations struggle to keep pace with rapidly advancing technologies like generative AI and autonomous systems.

A global survey by Oxford Insights (2024) found regulatory disparities to be the top governance challenge cited by 73% of multinational organizations implementing AI for sustainability.

Nemitz (2018) argues that effective enforcement requires not just robust legal frameworks but also sufficiently resourced regulatory bodies with technical expertise—resources often lacking even in advanced economies and severely constrained in developing regions.

5.6.2   Corporate Implementation Barriers

Companies face several challenges in implementing robust AI governance:

- **Resource Constraints**: Smaller organizations often lack dedicated expertise and tools for comprehensive governance.
- **Competitive Pressures**: Time-to-market considerations sometimes conflict with thorough ethical review processes, creating tension between business and governance objectives.
- **Skills Gaps**: Insufficient AI ethics expertise within organizations, with a global shortage of qualified professionals who understand both technical systems and ethical implications.
- **Governance Integration**: Difficulty integrating AI governance into existing corporate structures and processes, particularly when sustainability and technology functions operate separately.

Research by Deloitte (2024) indicates that organizations with integrated governance approaches—linking AI ethics directly with sustainability objectives—demonstrate 56% more effective implementation and 43% higher stakeholder satisfaction.

As William Janeway (2025)[5] notes, trust is not an abstract ethical add-on—it is the currency of sustainable AI adoption. Even the most technically advanced systems will face resistance unless public trust is actively cultivated through transparency, inclusion, and accountability mechanisms.

Kaminski and Malgieri (2021) note that corporate implementation barriers often stem from inadequate incentive structures that fail to reward ethical AI development, creating tension between short-term business objectives and longer-term ethical considerations.

---

[5] William H. Janeway, "What Trust Means in an Uncertain World," *Project Syndicate*, February 2025, https://www.project-syndicate.org/onpoint/what-trust-means-in-uncertain-world-by-william-h-janeway-2025-02.

5.6.3   Evolving AI Risks

AI capabilities continue to develop rapidly, creating new governance challenges:

- **Generative AI**: Systems creating realistic content raise concerns about misinformation, manipulation, and unauthorized representation.
- **Autonomous Decision Systems**: Increasing autonomy raises questions about accountability when systems make consequential sustainability decisions.
- **Systemic and Emergent Risks**: Complex AI systems interacting with each other and the environment can create unforeseen consequences that governance frameworks must anticipate.

A study by the Stanford AI Index (2024) indicates that governance frameworks typically lag 18–24 months behind technological advancements, creating temporary governance gaps for cutting-edge applications.

Dafoe (2018) argues that these evolving risks necessitate governance approaches that can anticipate and adapt to emergent challenges rather than simply responding to known issues, requiring more sophisticated risk assessment methodologies than those currently deployed in most organizations.

5.7   Future Governance Strategies

To address these challenges, several forward-looking governance approaches show promise:

5.7.1   Adaptive Governance Models

Traditional regulations often struggle to keep pace with AI innovation. Adaptive models offer alternatives:

- **Regulatory Sandboxes**: Controlled environments where innovative solutions can be tested under regulatory supervision before wider deployment.

- **Performance-Based Standards**: Focusing on required outcomes rather than specific technical approaches, allowing flexibility in implementation while maintaining ethical standards.
- **Iterative Governance**: Regular review and revision cycles that adjust requirements based on emerging technologies and observed impacts.

The UK's Financial Conduct Authority pioneering such approaches reports 67% faster innovation cycles while maintaining strong ethical standards (Financial Conduct Authority, 2024).

Marchant and Wallach (2015) describe these approaches as "governance coordination", where multiple mechanisms including formal regulations, industry standards, and professional norms work together to create adaptive oversight systems more responsive to technological change than traditional command-and-control regulation.

5.7.2   Cross-Border Harmonization Efforts

Initiatives to reduce regulatory fragmentation include:

- **Equivalence Frameworks**: Mechanisms for recognizing compliance with one regime as sufficient for another when core principles align.
- **Global Technical Standards**: Development of common technical specifications that embed ethical considerations and can be referenced by multiple regulatory systems.
- **Collaborative Enforcement**: Coordination between national regulators to address cross-border AI applications consistently.

The G7 Hiroshima AI Process initiated in 2023 represents a significant step toward creating common international approaches to AI governance (G7, 2024).

Bradford (2020) describes the process of regulatory convergence as the "Brussels Effect", where influential regulatory regimes like the EU's create de facto global standards as organizations adopt the most stringent requirements to ensure global compliance, potentially offering a path toward harmonization despite fragmented formal governance.

5.7.3   Inclusive Governance Development

Ensuring governance reflects diverse perspectives:

- **Multistakeholder Processes**: Involving civil society, affected communities, and diverse experts in governance development.
- **Indigenous and Traditional Knowledge**: Incorporating Non-Western ethical frameworks and governance approaches.
- **Accessibility Considerations**: Ensuring governance mechanisms themselves don't create barriers to participation.

Research by the Alan Turing Institute (2024) demonstrates that inclusive governance processes result in AI systems with 58% fewer unintended consequences when deployed in diverse communities.

Mohamed et al. (2020) argue that decolonial approaches to AI governance are essential for creating truly inclusive frameworks that reflect diverse cultural perspectives rather than imposing Western ethical norms globally, particularly important for sustainability applications affecting diverse communities and ecosystems.

Building on this, McCourt (2024)[6] stresses the importance of decentralized digital governance to safeguard individual data rights and prevent AI from being weaponized for corporate surveillance. He calls for:

- **Digital Property Rights**: Giving individuals control over how their personal data is collected, used, and monetized.
- **Decentralized Infrastructure**: Avoiding over-reliance on dominant tech platforms by promoting distributed systems for AI development and deployment.
- **Transparent AI Governance**: Ensuring that AI-driven decisions remain explainable, accountable, and open to public scrutiny.

These principles complement emerging global initiatives like the EU AI Act and the UN Digital Public Goods Alliance, which aim to democratize access to AI while enforcing ethical safeguards.

Real-world examples highlight the consequences of ignoring these principles:

---

[6] Willy McCourt, *Digital Infrastructure and Public Value: Reclaiming the Platform State* (Oxford: Oxford University Press, 2024).

Amazon's AI Recruiter[7]: Amazon developed an AI hiring tool that was eventually scrapped after it was found to discriminate against women. Trained on biased historical hiring data, the system consistently downgraded résumés that included the word "women's", exemplifying how opaque systems can perpetuate harmful biases. Twitter's AI Image Cropping[8]: Twitter's image-cropping algorithm was discovered to preferentially center white faces over Black ones. The company shut down the feature after public backlash, underscoring the critical need for inclusive design and pre-deployment auditing of AI systems Vincent (2021).

5.8 Conclusion: Establishing a Responsible AI Future

For AI to drive sustainable development responsibly, businesses and governments must prioritize:

- **Robust AI governance frameworks** ensuring fairness, transparency, and accountability.
- **Ethical AI policies** mitigating bias and safeguarding data privacy.
- **Collaborative international AI regulation** fostering innovation while addressing risks.
- **Inclusive approaches** ensuring AI benefits are widely distributed.

The governance approaches outlined in this chapter provide a foundation for responsible AI implementation. By aligning governance with sustainability objectives, organizations can ensure their AI deployments contribute positively to both business objectives and broader social and environmental goals.

As AI capabilities continue to advance, governance frameworks must evolve correspondingly. The organizations and societies that successfully

---

[7] Jeffrey Dastin, "Amazon Scraps Secret AI Recruiting Tool That Showed Bias Against Women," *Reuters*, October 10, 2018. https://www.reuters.com/article/us-amazon-com-jobs-automation-insight-idUSKCN1MK08G.

[8] James Vincent, "Twitter Apologizes for Racial Bias in Image Cropping Algorithm," *The Verge*, May 19, 2021. https://www.theverge.com/2021/5/19/22442915/twitter-apology-image-cropping-algorithm-bias-racial-white-faces.

navigate this complex landscape will be those that view governance not as a constraint but as an enabler of responsible innovation that creates lasting value.

REFERENCES

AI Transparency Institute. (2024). *Global survey on explainable AI adoption and impact*. AI Transparency Publications.

Akbar, Y. H., & Ebibi, M. (2021). AI policy transfer between emerging economies: The case of Egypt and the UAE. *Technology in Society, 67*, Article 101703.

Alan Turing Institute. (2024). *Inclusive AI governance: Effectiveness study*. Alan Turing Institute Publications.

Arora, P. (2019). *The next billion users: Digital life beyond the West*. Harvard University Press.

Autor, D., Chin, C., Salomons, A. M., & Seegmiller, B. (2022). *New frontiers: The origins and content of new work, 1940–2018*. NBER Working Paper No. 30389. National Bureau of Economic Research. https://doi.org/10.3386/w30389

Bradford, A. (2020). *The Brussels effect: How the European Union rules the world*. Oxford University Press.

Branger, F., Ponssard, J. P., Sartor, O., & Sato, M. (2015). EU ETS, free allocations, and activity level thresholds: The devil lies in the details. *Journal of the Association of Environmental and Resource Economists, 2*(3), 401–437.

Cihon, P., Maas, M. M., & Kemp, L. (2021). Should artificial intelligence governance be centralized? Design lessons from history. In *Proceedings of the 2021 AAAI/ACM Conference on AI, Ethics, and Society* (pp. 228–237).

Cohen, A., & Nissim, K. (2020). Towards formalizing the GDPR's notion of singling out. *Proceedings of the National Academy of Sciences, 117*(15), 8344–8352.

Dafoe, A. (2018). *AI governance: A research agenda*. Governance of AI Program, Future of Humanity Institute, University of Oxford.

Dastin, J. (2018). Amazon scraps secret AI recruiting tool that showed bias against women. *Reuters*. October 10, 2018. https://www.reuters.com/article/us-amazon-com-jobs-automation-insight-idUSKCN1MK08G

Deloitte. (2024). *AI governance integration and implementation outcomes*. Deloitte Research.

e-Estonia Briefing Centre. (2023). *Estonia's AI and open digital governance*. https://e-estonia.com/solutions/e-governance/

European Commission. (2024). *The AI Act: Regulating artificial intelligence for societal impact*. EU Policy Report.

Financial Conduct Authority. (2023). *Algorithmic bias in financial services*. UK Government Publications.

Financial Conduct Authority. (2024). *Regulatory sandboxes and financial innovation: Five-year impact assessment*. UK Government Publications.

Floridi, L., & Cowls, J. (2019). A unified framework of five principles for AI in society. *Harvard Data Science Review, 1*(1).

G7. (2024). *Hiroshima AI process: Progress report*. G7 Publications.

Hagendorff, T. (2020). The ethics of AI ethics: An evaluation of guidelines. *Minds and Machines, 30*(1), 99–120.

IBM Security. (2024). *Data protection and privacy in AI systems*. IBM Research.

International Monetary Fund. (2024). *AI adoption in developing economies: Strategies for inclusive growth*. IMF Staff Discussion Note SDN/24/03. https://www.imf.org/en/Publications/Staff-Discussion-Notes/AI-developing-economies

Janeway, W. H. (2025). What trust means in an uncertain world. *Project Syndicate*. February 2025. https://www.project-syndicate.org/onpoint/what-trust-means-in-uncertain-world-by-william-h-janeway-2025-02

Kaminski, M. E., & Malgieri, G. (2021). Algorithmic impact assessments under the GDPR: Producing multi-layered explanations. *International Data Privacy Law, 11*(2), 125–144.

Kleinberg, J., Ludwig, J., Mullainathan, S., & Sunstein, C. R. (2018). Discrimination in the age of algorithms. *Journal of Legal Analysis, 10*, 113–174.

KPMG. (2024). *Global survey of AI regulatory compliance*. KPMG International.

LinkedIn Economic Graph. (2024). *Future of work report: AI skills and job market trends*. LinkedIn Corporation. https://economicgraph.linkedin.com/research/future-of-work-report-ai

Marchant, G. E., & Wallach, W. (2015). Coordinating technology governance. *Issues in Science and Technology, 31*(4), 43–50.

Martin, K. (2019). Ethical implications and accountability of algorithms. *Journal of Business Ethics, 160*(4), 835–850.

McCourt, W. (2024). *Digital infrastructure and public value: Reclaiming the platform state*. Oxford University Press.

MIT Work of the Future Task Force. (2024). *Human-AI collaboration in the workplace: Performance outcomes and design principles*. Massachusetts Institute of Technology. https://workofthefuture.mit.edu/research/human-ai-collaboration

Mohamed, S., Png, M. T., & Isaac, W. (2020). Decolonial AI: Decolonial theory as sociotechnical foresight in artificial intelligence. *Philosophy & Technology, 33*(4), 659–684.

Mohieldin, M. (2024). Governing AI. *Al-Ahram Weekly*. February 2024. https://english.ahram.org.eg/News/508878.aspx

Mulgan, G. (2021). The case for exploratory governance. *Nature Sustainability,* *4*(6), 459–461.

Nemitz, P. (2018). Constitutional democracy and technology in the age of artificial intelligence. *Philosophical Transactions of the Royal Society A: Mathematical, Physical and Engineering Sciences, 376*(2133), 20180089.

Nield, D. (2024). DALL-E vs. Stable diffusion: What's the difference? *TechRadar.* January 15, 2024. https://www.techradar.com/news/dall-e-vs-stable-diffusion

OECD. (2024). *AI governance and ethical considerations.* OECD Publications.

Oxford Insights. (2024). *Government AI readiness index.* Oxford University Press.

PwC. (2024). *AI ethics in corporate governance.* PricewaterhouseCoopers.

Raghavan, M., Barocas, S., Kleinberg, J., & Levy, K. (2020). Mitigating bias in algorithmic hiring: Evaluating claims and practices. In *Proceedings of the 2020 Conference on Fairness, Accountability, and Transparency* (pp. 469–481).

Roberts, H., Cowls, J., Morley, J., Taddeo, M., Wang, V., & Floridi, L. (2021). The Chinese approach to artificial intelligence: An analysis of policy, ethics, and regulation. *AI & Society, 36*(1), 59–77.

Rodrik, D. (2015). Premature deindustrialization. *Journal of Economic Growth, 21*(1), 1–33. https://doi.org/10.1007/s10887-015-9122-3

Smuha, N. A. (2021). From a 'race to AI' to a 'race to AI regulation': Regulatory competition for artificial intelligence. *Law, Innovation and Technology, 13*(1), 57–84.

Stanford AI Index. (2024). *Global AI governance trends analysis.* Stanford University.

UNCTAD. (2024). *Digital economy report: AI governance in developing nations.* United Nations Conference on Trade and Development.

UNDP. (2024). *AI governance capacity building: Global assessment.* United Nations Development Programme.

United Nations. (2024). *UN Secretary-General's roadmap for digital cooperation: Implementation report.* United Nations Publications.

Vincent, J. (2021). Twitter apologizes for racial bias in image cropping algorithm. *The Verge.* May 19, 2021. https://www.theverge.com/2021/5/19/22442915/twitter-apology-image-cropping-algorithm-bias-racial-white-faces

Wachter, S., Mittelstadt, B., & Floridi, L. (2017). Transparent, explainable, and accountable AI for robotics. *Science Robotics, 2*(6), eaan6080.

World Economic Forum. (2024). *Global AI governance and policy analysis.* World Economic Forum.

CHAPTER 6

AI and Workforce Transformation—Opportunities and Challenges

Abstract The rise of AI-driven automation is reshaping labor markets worldwide, impacting workforce skills, employment structures, and job creation dynamics. While AI offers opportunities to enhance productivity and innovation, it also raises concerns about job displacement and skills gaps. This chapter explores the dual impact of AI on the workforce, examines reskilling strategies, and discusses policy interventions needed to ensure an inclusive and sustainable transition. Drawing on global case studies and empirical evidence, we provide insights for managing workforce transformation across diverse economic contexts.

Keywords AI and employment · Workforce automation · Reskilling · Future of work · AI policy · Labor market transformation · Human-AI collaboration

6.1   Introduction: The Changing Nature of Work in the AI Era

Artificial Intelligence is accelerating workplace transformations, influencing how businesses operate and how workers adapt to new roles. The shift toward AI-driven economies requires an understanding of:

- The **opportunities AI presents** for job enhancement and efficiency.
- The **challenges of workforce displacement** and skills obsolescence.
- The **policy measures** needed to ensure a fair transition.

According to the International Labour Organization (2024), AI technologies will affect approximately 85% of global jobs in some form by 2030, though the nature and degree of impact will vary significantly across regions, industries, and skill levels. This dramatic shift demands careful examination of how societies can manage workforce transitions to ensure that technological advancements translate into broadly shared benefits rather than exacerbating inequalities.

As Andrew Hill of the Financial Times[1] argues, the rise of generative AI is redefining the role of managers—not eliminating them, but repositioning them as evaluators, facilitators, and caretakers of displaced workers. Hill notes that modern leadership must balance the promise of productivity gains with empathy, ethics, and the preservation of workplace trust.

This transformation is not unprecedented—technological shifts have reshaped labor markets throughout history. However, as Brynjolfsson and McAfee (2014) note, AI-driven automation differs from previous waves of technological change in its pace, scope, and ability to affect cognitive as well as manual tasks, creating both more profound opportunities and more significant disruption.

This chapter examines the changing labor landscape, providing insights into AI's workforce impact across various sectors and offering evidence-based approaches for managing workforce transitions effectively.

---

[1] Andrew Hill, "AI Will Transform Your Role as a Manager. Here's How," *Financial Times*, March 2024. https://www.ft.com/content/

6.2   AI's Impact on Jobs: A Dual Perspective

AI's influence on employment is multifaceted, bringing both **automation risks** and **new job creation opportunities**.

However, as McCourt (2024)[2] cautions, the growing dominance of a handful of digital monopolies could shape AI-driven labor markets in ways that restrict, rather than expand, economic mobility. By controlling critical AI infrastructures, large corporations are increasingly able to dictate employment patterns, stifling competition and undermining digital independence—particularly in developing economies.

To counter these dynamics, McCourt calls for structural reforms including data ownership rights and decentralized AI platforms, emphasizing the need to design AI transitions that empower individuals instead of reinforcing corporate control.

Real-world examples illustrate how market concentration impacts employment opportunities:

- *Microsoft & OpenAI Partnership*[3]: Microsoft's $10 billion investment in OpenAI granted it privileged access to GPT-4, limiting broader market access to advanced generative AI and reducing opportunities for smaller competitors and startups.
- *Google's AI Search Integration*[4]: Google's use of proprietary AI in search results favors its own services, creating barriers for other platforms and shaping the digital labor ecosystem in ways that prioritize corporate interests over open market competition.

6.2.1   Job Displacement and Automation Risks

AI and automation technologies are increasingly capable of performing tasks that were previously the exclusive domain of human workers:

---

[2] Willy McCourt, *Digital Infrastructure and Public Value: Reclaiming the Platform State* (Oxford: Oxford University Press, 2024).

[3] Cade Metz, "Microsoft Invests $10 Billion in OpenAI, Extending Partnership," *The New York Times*, January 23, 2023. https://www.nytimes.com/2023/01/23/technology/microsoft-invests-openai.html.

[4] Natasha Lomas, "Google's AI-Boosted Search Draws Regulatory Scrutiny," *TechCrunch*, August 2023. https://techcrunch.com/2023/08/04/google-ai-search-eu-regulation.

- **Repetitive Task Automation**: Roles in manufacturing, retail, and customer service face significant transformation, with 45% of activities in these sectors technically automatable today (McKinsey Global Institute, 2024).
- **AI-Driven Decision-Making**: Middle-management and administrative positions in finance, law, and business services are experiencing disruption, with 38% of tasks potentially automatable (PwC, 2024).
- **Algorithmic Efficiencies**: Logistics, supply chains, and transportation are being reshaped by AI optimization, affecting 42% of current roles in these sectors (World Economic Forum, 2024).

Research by the Oxford Martin School (2024) suggests that approximately 47% of U.S. employment, 35% of UK jobs, and varying percentages in other economies are at high risk of automation within the next two decades. However, these estimates focus on technical feasibility rather than actual implementation, which is influenced by economic, social, and regulatory factors.

Autor et al. (2022) emphasize that automation typically targets specific tasks rather than entire occupations, creating opportunities for job transformation rather than simple replacement. This nuanced view suggests that while few jobs may be entirely automated, many will be substantially reconfigured.

Case Study: AI in Manufacturing (Germany)

The implementation of AI-powered robotic systems in German automotive factories provides insights into real-world automation impacts:

- 30% reduction in assembly line workers over 3 years
- Creation of new technical roles in AI maintenance and programming
- Net employment change of −18% (job losses exceeding new positions)
- 35% productivity improvement in affected production lines
- Significant wage premium (40–70%) for workers who successfully transitioned to AI-related roles

The company implemented a substantial reskilling program, with 65% of displaced workers successfully transitioning to new roles within the organization, while others either retired or moved to different sectors (OECD, 2024).

This case aligns with Dauth et al.'s (2021) research on industrial robots in Germany, which found that while robots displace some manufacturing workers, the net impact on total employment may be limited due to productivity gains and new job creation in supporting roles.

The varying impact of AI and automation technologies across different economic sectors reflects both technical feasibility and economic incentives for implementation. Table 6.1 summarizes current estimates of automation potential, projected job displacement, and new role creation across major economic sectors, highlighting the uneven distribution of workforce transformation.

6.2.2 AI as a Job Creator

While automation risks are significant, AI is also generating new employment opportunities:

- **New AI-Specific Roles**: Positions in AI development, ethics, data science, and machine learning engineering are growing at 17% annually, significantly outpacing overall job market growth (LinkedIn Economic Graph, 2024).
- **Hybrid Human-AI Work**: Collaborative models where AI handles routine aspects while humans provide judgment, creativity, and emotional intelligence are emerging across industries, creating new role categories.
- **Enhanced Productivity Opportunities**: As AI increases productivity, it can create economic growth that generates new employment, particularly in scenarios where cost savings are reinvested in business expansion.
- **Entrepreneurship Enablement**: AI tools are democratizing capabilities previously available only to large organizations, enabling small businesses and entrepreneurs to compete more effectively.

Research by Deloitte (2024) indicates that for every job displaced by AI, approximately 1.2 new jobs are created in the global economy

Table 6.1 Automation potential and job transformation across major economic sectors

Economic sector	Technical automation potential (%)	Projected job displacement by 2030	New role creation potential	Key skills for emerging roles
Manufacturing	60–75	20–30% of current workforce	Moderate (0.8 new roles per displaced role)	AI systems maintenance, advanced manufacturing, human–robot collaboration
Financial services	40–55	15–25% of current workforce	High (1.5 new roles per displaced role)	Algorithm design, data ethics, client relationship management, financial technology
Healthcare	25–35	10–15% of administrative roles	Very High (2.3 new roles per displaced role)	AI diagnostics supervision, patient counseling, medical data science, care coordination
Retail & customer service	45–60	30–40% of current workforce	Low-Moderate (0.7 new roles per displaced role)	Experience design, personalization specialists, omnichannel management
Transportation & logistics	55–70	25–35% of current workforce	Moderate (0.9 new roles per displaced role)	Autonomous systems management, complex logistics planning, last-mile specialization

(continued)

Table 6.1 (continued)

Economic sector	Technical automation potential (%)	Projected job displacement by 2030	New role creation potential	Key skills for emerging roles
Professional services	30–40	15–20% of current workforce	High (1.6 new roles per displaced role)	AI-augmented consulting, knowledge management, specialized expert roles
Education	20–30	5–15% of current workforce	High (1.8 new roles per displaced role)	Adaptive learning design, educational content creation, personalized coaching
Construction	30–40	10–20% of current workforce	Moderate (1.0 new roles per displaced role)	AI-assisted design, robotic system management, complex installation skills

Source Compiled from McKinsey Global Institute (2024), PwC (2024), and World Economic Forum (2024) data

overall—though this ratio varies significantly by region, from 1.8:1 in advanced economies to 0.7:1 in some developing regions.

As Acemoglu and Restrepo (2019) observe, the net employment impact of automation technologies depends critically on whether they primarily replace existing tasks or create new ones that require human workers. AI appears capable of both effects, with the balance varying across different applications and contexts.

Case Study: AI in Healthcare (United States)

The implementation of AI-assisted diagnostics in a major U.S. healthcare system demonstrates AI's job transformation potential:

- Radiologists' productivity increased by 32% through AI assistance in image interpretation.
- 24% reduction in diagnostic errors when using AI-human collaborative approach.
- New roles emerged for AI training specialists and medical data analysts.
- No radiologist positions were eliminated, but role focus shifted to higher-value activities.
- Overall employment in the system increased by 8% to support expanded services enabled by efficiency gains.

The health system invested significantly in retraining, with radiologists receiving 120+ hours of education on AI collaboration techniques over an 18-month transition period (American Medical Association, 2024).

This case exemplifies what Davenport and Kirby (2016) term "augmentation" rather than automation, where AI enhances human capabilities rather than replacing them, potentially creating more value than either humans or technology could achieve independently.

6.2.3   Regional and Demographic Variations in AI's Impact

AI's effects on labor markets vary substantially across regions and demographic groups:

Regional Disparities:

- **Advanced Economies**: Generally experiencing more balanced job displacement and creation, with significant variation by industry.
- **Emerging Economies**: Facing greater risk as automation may undermine comparative advantage in labor-intensive manufacturing.
- **Developing Economies**: Could experience "premature deindustrialization" as automation reduces the manufacturing employment pathway used historically by developed nations.

Demographic Considerations:

- **Gender Impact**: Initial research shows different patterns of AI impact across genders, with women overrepresented in some highly automatable roles but also in healthcare and education, which show greater resilience (ILO, 2024). As Mohieldin and Ramadan (2024)[5] note, *"digital inclusion strategies that overlook gender-specific barriers risk reinforcing, rather than narrowing, existing economic inequalities."* Their study emphasizes that empowering women through equitable access to digital infrastructure and skills is essential for inclusive AI-driven development in MENA.

- **Age Factors**: Workers over 50 often face greater challenges in transitioning to new roles, with retraining effectiveness decreasing with age in many contexts.
- **Educational Divides**: Workers with tertiary education generally face lower automation risk and greater opportunities in emerging roles.

A comprehensive study by the International Labour Organization (ILO, 2024) found that without intervention, AI-driven workforce changes could increase income inequality by 4.5% to 8% in advanced economies and 9% to 15% in developing economies by 2030.

Rodrik (2015) argues that these disparities reflect fundamental differences in industrial structure and institutional capacity across regions, with developing economies particularly vulnerable due to their reliance on labor-intensive manufacturing as a development pathway.

6.3 THE RESKILLING IMPERATIVE: PREPARING THE WORKFORCE FOR AI

The transition to an AI-driven economy requires significant investment in **reskilling and upskilling**. Governments, businesses, and educational institutions must collaborate to:

6.3.1 Identify Future Skill Requirements

Understanding emerging skill needs is essential for effective workforce development:

---

[5] Mahmoud Mohieldin and Racha Ramadan, *Could Digital Inclusion Close the Gender Economic Gap in the MENA Region?*, World Bank Policy Research Working Paper 10,531, January 2024.

- **Technical Skills**: Programming, data analysis, AI operations, and cybersecurity are experiencing rapidly growing demand, with vacancy rates exceeding 40% in many markets (World Economic Forum, 2024).
- **Human-Centric Skills**: As AI handles routine tasks, skills such as creativity, emotional intelligence, critical thinking, and complex problem-solving become increasingly valuable and automation-resistant.
- **Hybrid Skill Sets**: The most in-demand roles often combine technical understanding with domain expertise and soft skills, creating complex skill profiles that are challenging to develop through traditional education alone.

Research by the McKinsey Global Institute (2024) indicates that demand for advanced technological skills will rise by 90% by 2030, while the need for social and emotional skills will increase by 26%.

Bughin et al. (2018) emphasize that future skill needs are not simply about more technology expertise but rather about increasingly sophisticated combinations of technical, business, and interpersonal capabilities that enable effective human-AI collaboration.

The gap between emerging skill demands and current educational capacity represents a critical challenge for workforce development. Figure 6.1 highlights the projected imbalances between workforce demand and expected educational output across key AI-related skill categories, underscoring the need for targeted expansion in high-demand areas.

The bar chart above visualizes the gap between projected demand for AI-related skills and the expected educational output. It shows significant shortfalls across all categories, with the largest gaps in AI systems engineering (68% shortfall) and human-AI collaboration (66% shortfall), reinforcing our chapter's emphasis on the urgent need for reskilling initiatives.

6.3.2   Government-Led Workforce Reskilling Initiatives

Public sector approaches to workforce development vary significantly in scope and effectiveness:

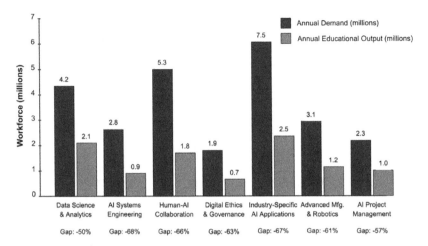

Fig. 6.1 Projected AI skills demand vs. Educational output by skill category (2025–2030). *Data source* Analysis based on data from World Economic Forum (2024), UNESCO (2024), and McKinsey Global Institute (2024)

- **Singapore's AI Workforce Strategy**: A comprehensive national program providing AI training subsidies for displaced workers, integrating private sector partnerships, and aligning education with industry needs.
- 92,000 workers trained in AI-related skills
- 78% successful placement rate in new roles
- Average 23% salary increase for program graduates
- **European Union's Digital Skills Agenda**: Coordinated approach across member states with dedicated funding for digital upskilling.
- €9.2 billion invested in digital skills programs
- Focus on both basic digital literacy and advanced AI capabilities
- Special provisions for vulnerable workers and regions
- **Canada's AI Skills for Mid-Career Transition**: Program specifically targeting workers aged 35–55 affected by automation.
- 70% completion rate for enrolled participants
- 65% employment in new roles within 6 months
- Emphasis on industry-specific AI applications

These government initiatives demonstrate the importance of strategic planning, adequate funding, and collaboration with industry and educational institutions (OECD, 2024).

Katz and Krueger (2017) note that successful public reskilling programs typically combine financial support for learners with systematic coordination between training providers and employers, ensuring that skills development aligns with actual labor market needs.

6.3.3   Corporate AI Training Programs

Businesses are increasingly investing in workforce development to meet their evolving skill needs:

- **Google's AI Certification Program**: Comprehensive curriculum designed to upskill both technical and non-technical employees.
- 185,000 employees trained globally
- 40% of participants from non-technical backgrounds
- 68% reporting enhanced job performance and career opportunities
- **IBM's AI Academy**: Corporate training initiative focused on practical AI skills development.
- 350,000 employees and clients trained
- Blended learning approach combining online and in-person instruction
- Role-specific learning paths based on job function
- **Amazon's Technical Apprenticeship**: Program retraining warehouse workers for technical roles including AI operations.
- 45% of participants from hourly workforce backgrounds
- 92% completion rate
- Average 65% increase in compensation post-program

According to PwC research (2024), companies that invest at least 5% of their AI implementation budgets in workforce training report 42% higher project success rates and 38% lower employee turnover during digital transformations.

Fuller et al. (2019) argue that corporate training programs are most effective when they create clear career pathways for workers, combining skill development with opportunities for advancement that provide both motivation and practical application contexts.

6.3.4   Educational System Transformation

Traditional education systems require significant adaptation to prepare workers for AI-transformed economies:

- **Curriculum Evolution**: Educational content must rapidly adapt to changing skill requirements, with 65% of current primary school students likely to work in roles that don't yet exist (World Economic Forum, 2024).
- **Lifelong Learning Models**: The traditional front-loaded education model is increasingly inadequate, necessitating systems that support continuous learning throughout careers.
- **Industry-Education Partnerships**: Closer collaboration between employers and educational institutions is essential to ensure relevance of training.

UNESCO (2024) reports that education systems that have successfully integrated AI-relevant skills show three common characteristics: agile curriculum development processes, strong industry connections, and embedded digital literacy from early education through higher learning.

Baker (2021) argues that fundamental reforms to educational financing and credentialing are needed to support lifelong learning in AI-transformed economies, including voucher systems, tax incentives, and alternative credentialing models that recognize continuous skill development.

6.4   The Future of Work: AI and Human Collaboration

While AI is automating many tasks, **human-AI collaboration models** are emerging as the future of work. These models focus on:

6.4.1   Augmentation Rather Than Replacement

The most successful AI implementations typically enhance human capabilities rather than simply replacing workers:

- **Augmenting Human Decision-Making**: AI provides insights and recommendations while humans apply judgment, contextual understanding, and ethical considerations.
- **Automating Routine Components**: AI handles repetitive or computational aspects of work, allowing humans to focus on higher-value activities.
- **Enabling Creativity and Innovation**: AI tools can expand human creative capabilities by generating options, testing scenarios, or handling technical aspects of creative production.

Research by MIT (2024) found that teams combining human and AI capabilities outperformed both AI-only and human-only approaches by 27% in complex problem-solving tasks across multiple domains.

This collaborative approach aligns with what Daugherty and Wilson (2018) call the "missing middle" of human-AI interaction, where neither full automation nor fully human work produces optimal results. Instead, carefully designed collaboration between humans and AI creates the greatest value.

6.4.2   Redefining Roles Around Human Comparative Advantage

As AI capabilities advance, human roles are evolving to emphasize uniquely human strengths:

- **Emotional Intelligence**: Roles requiring empathy, interpersonal understanding, and relationship management are proving resistant to automation.
- **Ethical Judgment**: Positions requiring value-based decision-making and ethical reasoning remain predominantly human domains.
- **Creativity and Innovation**: While AI can assist creative processes, conceptual creativity, and breakthrough innovation continue to rely heavily on human capabilities.
- **Complex Physical Skills**: Many trades and physical occupations combine dexterity, spatial awareness, and contextual judgment in ways that remain challenging to automate.

A Harvard Business Review study (2024) identified that roles emphasizing these human advantages experienced 60% less automation pressure compared to roles focused primarily on information processing or routine physical tasks.

Frey and Osborne (2017) note that tasks requiring high degrees of social perceptiveness, creativity, negotiation, and persuasion remain among the most resistant to automation, suggesting career pathways that emphasize these capabilities offer greater long-term security.

Case Study: AI-Augmented Customer Support (India)

A multinational bank deployed AI-powered chatbots to handle basic customer inquiries while transitioning human agents to more complex financial consultations:

- Basic queries (65% of total volume) handled by AI systems
- Human agents focused on complex financial advisory and relationship management
- Customer satisfaction increased by 40% for both AI and human interactions
- Employee satisfaction improved by 35% as agents engaged in more meaningful work
- Overall service capacity increased by g 180% while employment remained stable
- Average agent compensation increased by 28% as role complexity increased

The transition included a comprehensive 12-week training program for all customer service representatives, with 92% successfully adapting to new advisory roles (Deloitte, 2023).

This case demonstrates what Susskind and Susskind (2015) describe as "task encroachment" rather than wholesale job replacement, where technology gradually transforms occupations by handling routine tasks while creating opportunities for humans to provide higher-value services.

6.4.3 Hybrid Working Models and Digital Labor Platforms

AI is also transforming where and how work is performed:

- **Remote Work Enablement**: AI tools are supporting distributed work by enhancing communication, project management, and virtual collaboration.
- **Digital Labor Platforms**: AI-powered platforms are creating new forms of work organization, from gig economy matching to specialized professional services.
- **Global Talent Access**: AI-enabled translation, collaboration, and work monitoring tools are facilitating cross-border work arrangements.

According to McKinsey (2024), these emerging work models could make 20–30% of the global workforce potentially available for remote engagement by 2030, significantly reshaping labor markets and economic geography.

Schwellnus et al. (2019) note that these changes may fundamentally transform employment relationships, creating both opportunities for greater flexibility and autonomy as well as risks of decreased employment security and benefits—policy responses must carefully balance these considerations.

6.5   Policy Recommendations for a Just Transition

To ensure AI benefits all workers, policymakers must implement regulatory measures that:

6.5.1   Strengthen Education and Training Systems

- **Modernize Education**: Update curricula at all levels to incorporate digital literacy, AI understanding, and human-centric skills resistant to automation.
- **Expand Access to Continuous Learning**: Develop systems supporting lifelong education, including funding mechanisms, recognition of non-traditional learning, and flexible delivery models.
- **Target Vulnerable Workers**: Provide special support for demographics and regions at higher risk of displacement, including dedicated retraining funds and transition assistance.

The World Bank (2024) estimates that countries investing at least 1.5% of GDP in education and training specifically focused on technological transition achieve 40% better employment outcomes during periods of technological disruption.

Goldin and Katz (2010) emphasize that broader educational access has historically been the most effective response to technological disruption, suggesting that policies that democratize educational opportunity are crucial for ensuring AI-driven prosperity is widely shared.

6.5.2 Adapt Social Protection Systems

- **Modernize Safety Nets**: Ensure unemployment, healthcare, and retirement systems accommodate changing work patterns, including gig work and frequent transitions.
- **Consider New Models**: Explore innovative approaches such as portable benefits, skill development accounts, or forms of basic income to address gaps in traditional employment-based systems.
- **Support Geographic Mobility**: Develop programs to assist workers in relocating from declining to growing regions, including housing assistance and family support services.

OECD research (2024) shows that countries with comprehensive social protection systems experience 35% less economic hardship during technology-driven transitions and 28% faster workforce adaptation.

Standing (2017) argues that emerging work patterns in AI-driven economies may require fundamental rethinking of social protection systems, moving beyond employment-based models toward citizenship-based approaches that provide security regardless of work status.

6.5.3 Promote Ethical AI Development and Deployment

- **Require Impact Assessments**: Mandate evaluation of workforce impacts before large-scale AI implementation, particularly in high-employment sectors.
- **Encourage Participatory Design**: Promote worker involvement in designing and implementing AI systems that will affect their roles.

- **Develop Fair Transition Standards**: Establish guidelines for responsible automation that includes adequate notice, retraining opportunities, and consideration of broader social impacts.

The European Commission (2024) reports that companies implementing ethical AI deployment processes experience 45% higher workforce acceptance and 37% less implementation disruption compared to those taking purely technical approaches.

Lee et al. (2019) note that participatory approaches to AI development not only increase acceptance but also typically result in more effective systems, as worker domain knowledge improves design and implementation outcomes when properly incorporated.

6.5.4   *Foster New Economic Opportunities*

- **Support Entrepreneurship**: Develop programs helping workers leverage AI tools to create their own opportunities, including business development services and startup funding.
- **Invest in Growth Sectors**: Target public investment toward industries with job creation potential that complements AI capabilities.
- **Enable SME Adoption**: Provide resources helping small and medium enterprises adopt AI productivity tools while maintaining or growing employment.

Research by the World Economic Forum (2024) indicates that regions with coordinated strategies for AI adoption and job creation demonstrate 40% better employment outcomes than those focusing solely on either technology adoption or job preservation.

Mazzucato (2021) emphasizes the importance of mission-oriented public investment in creating new economic opportunities, suggesting that governments should strategically direct resources toward areas where AI can address social challenges while creating quality employment.

6.6   REGIONAL APPROACHES TO AI WORKFORCE TRANSFORMATION

Different regions face distinct challenges and are developing varied approaches to workforce transition.

Very Low
(20-40)

High (70-
80)

Very High
(80-90)

Low (40-60)

Fig. 6.2 Global AI workforce readiness index by region. 2024 *Source* Analysis based on data from OECD (2024), World Bank (2024), and ILO (). Map by Ultimaps

Regional variations in AI workforce readiness reflect complex differences in educational systems, digital infrastructure, policy frameworks, and labor market structures. Figure 6.2 illustrates the current state of AI workforce readiness across global regions, incorporating measures of technical training capacity, social protection adequacy, and labor market flexibility.

6.6.1 Advanced Economies

- **Focus on Reskilling Advanced Workforces**: Countries like Germany, Japan, and South Korea emphasize maintaining technological leadership while transitioning specialized workers to new roles.
- **Managing Demographic Challenges**: Aging populations in many advanced economies mean automation may help address labor shortages rather than primarily causing unemployment.
- **Strong Policy Frameworks**: Typically feature robust social protection and educational systems that can be adapted for AI workforce transitions, though often require significant modernization.

6.6.2   Emerging Economies

- **Balancing Manufacturing and Services Transitions**: Countries like China, Malaysia, and Brazil are navigating automation in manufacturing while developing service sector opportunities.
- **Building Technical Capability**: Significant investments in STEM education and digital infrastructure aim to ensure participation in higher-value AI economy roles.
- **Leveraging Demographic Advantages**: Younger populations provide adaptability advantages if educational systems can rapidly evolve.

6.6.3   Developing Economies

- **Seeking Development Pathways**: Nations with limited industrialization face challenges as traditional labor-intensive manufacturing pathways may narrow due to automation.
- **Digital Leapfrogging Opportunities**: Some regions may bypass traditional development stages using digital platforms and AI-enabled services.
- **Infrastructure and Education Gaps**: Limited digital infrastructure and educational capacity create substantial barriers to workforce adaptation.

The International Monetary Fund (2024) suggests that developing economies may need to pursue "inclusion-first" AI strategies that prioritize broad-based skills development and infrastructure access before advanced AI adoption in key sectors.

Rodrik (2018) argues that developing nations may need to reconsider traditional export-led manufacturing as a development pathway, instead seeking industries where human capabilities remain complementary to automation technologies or where limited automation may still provide comparative advantage.

The effectiveness of reskilling initiatives varies substantially based on program design, participant demographics, and implementation context. Table 6.2 compares outcomes across different reskilling approaches, highlighting key success factors and limitations that should inform future workforce development strategies.

Table 6.2 Comparative analysis of AI workforce reskilling programs

Program type	Program duration	Completion rate (%)	Employment rate (6 Months Post-Completion) (%)	Average wage change (%)	Key success factors	Primary limitations
Government-funded general digital skills	3–6 months	65–70	55–60	+12–18	Accessibility, broad applicability	Limited specialization, slower wage growth
Industry-Led technical certification	6–12 months	75–82	80–85	+25–40	Direct employer involvement, job-specific training	Higher barriers to entry, limited transferability
University-corporate partnerships	12–24 months	85–90	75–80	+30–45	Theoretical depth, practical application	Time commitment, higher costs
Online self-paced learning	1–12 months	15–25	30–40	+5–15	Flexibility, low cost, accessibility	Low completion rates, limited guidance
Apprenticeship programs	12–36 months	80–90	85–95	+40–60	Earn while learning, direct skill application	Limited scale, industry-specific
Rapid Bootcamp models	2–4 months	70–80	65–75	+15–30	Intensive immersion, quick workforce reentry	Limited depth, focuses on narrow skill sets
Internal corporate retraining	3–9 months	85–95	90–95 (retention)	+15–25	Job security, clear role pathways	Limited to existing employees, company-specific

Source Combined analysis of data from LinkedIn Economic Graph (2024), OECD (2024), and Deloitte (2024)

6.7   Conclusion: Building an AI-Ready Workforce

AI is transforming the global workforce, creating **both challenges and opportunities**. Preparing for this shift requires:

- **Investing in reskilling and education** that prepares workers not just for today's AI applications but for ongoing technological evolution.
- **Fostering human-AI collaboration models** that leverage the complementary strengths of people and technology.
- **Developing policies that balance innovation with workforce security** and ensure the benefits of AI are broadly shared.
- **Creating differentiated strategies** that address the specific workforce contexts of different regions and demographic groups.

By proactively addressing these priorities, societies can navigate the AI transition in ways that enhance economic productivity while maintaining social cohesion and expanding opportunity. The evidence presented in this chapter demonstrates that with appropriate preparation and policy frameworks, AI can contribute to more prosperous and inclusive economies rather than exacerbate inequalities.

References

Acemoglu, D., & Restrepo, P. (2019). Automation and new tasks: How technology displaces and reinstates labor. *Journal of Economic Perspectives, 33*(2), 3–30. https://doi.org/10.1257/jep.33.2.3

American Medical Association. (2024). AI in medical practice: Workforce impacts and adaptation. AMA Digital Health Research.

Autor, D. H. (2022). The labor market impacts of technological change: From unbridled enthusiasm to qualified optimism to vast uncertainty. *Journal of Economic Perspectives, 36*(4), 3–30. https://doi.org/10.1257/jep.36.4.3

Autor, D., Chin, C., Salomons, A. M., & Seegmiller, B. (2022). *New frontiers: The origins and content of new work, 1940–2018.* NBER Working Paper No. 30389. National Bureau of Economic Research. https://doi.org/10.3386/w30389

Baker, T. (2021). Lifelong learning in the age of AI: Restructuring educational financing for the digital era. *Journal of Education Policy, 36*(3), 412–435. https://doi.org/10.1080/02680939.2020.1819566

Breznitz, D., Orr, L., & de Vasconcelos, F. (2021). *Shaping the future of work in a digital world*. University of Toronto Innovation Policy Lab Working Paper.

Brynjolfsson, E., & McAfee, A. (2014). *The second machine age: Work, progress, and prosperity in a time of brilliant technologies*. W.W. Norton & Company.

Bughin, J., Hazan, E., Lund, S., Dahlström, P., Wiesinger, A., & Subramaniam, A. (2018). *Skill shift: Automation and the future of the workforce*. McKinsey Global Institute.

Chandrasekar, S., Devarajan, T., & Sundaresan, L. (2022). Bridging the gap: AI workforce development in emerging economies. *Journal of Development Economics, 155*, Article 102739. https://doi.org/10.1016/j.jdeveco.2021.102739

Daugherty, P. R., & Wilson, H. J. (2018). *Human + machine: Reimagining work in the age of AI*. Harvard Business Review Press.

Dauth, W., Findeisen, S., Südekum, J., & Woessner, N. (2021). The adjustment of labor markets to robots. *Journal of the European Economic Association, 19*(6), 3104–3153. https://doi.org/10.1093/jeea/jvab012

Davenport, T. H., & Kirby, J. (2016). *Only humans need apply: Winners and losers in the age of smart machines*. Harper Business.

Deloitte. (2023). *Global AI adoption survey: Workforce impacts and organizational responses*. Deloitte Research.

Deloitte. (2024). *AI job displacement and creation analysis: Global economic impacts*. Deloitte Global Research.

European Commission. (2024). *Ethical AI deployment and workforce acceptance*. EU Research Publications.

Frey, C. B., & Osborne, M. A. (2017). The future of employment: How susceptible are jobs to computerisation? *Technological Forecasting and Social Change, 114*, 254–280. https://doi.org/10.1016/j.techfore.2016.08.019

Fuller, J. B., et al. (2019). *Building the on-demand workforce*. Harvard Business School.

Gentilini, U., Almenfi, M., & Dale, P. (2020). *Social protection and jobs responses to COVID-19: A real-time review of country measures*. World Bank.

Goldin, C., & Katz, L. F. (2010). *The race between education and technology*. Harvard University Press.

Graham, M., & Hjorth, I. (2020). *Digital labour and development: Impacts of global digital labour platforms on developing economies*. Oxford Internet Institute Working Paper.

Hagendorff, T. (2020). The ethics of AI ethics: An evaluation of guidelines. *Minds and Machines, 30*, 99–120. https://doi.org/10.1007/s11023-020-09517-8

Hallward-Driemeier, M., & Nayyar, G. (2018). *Trouble in the making? The future of manufacturing-led development*. World Bank.

Hill, A. (2024). AI will transform your role as a manager. Here's how. *Financial Times*. https://www.ft.com/content/

International Labour Organization. (2024). *The future of work in the age of AI: Employment trends and policy responses*. ILO Publications.

International Monetary Fund. (2024). *AI adoption in developing economies: Strategies for inclusive growth*. IMF Staff Discussion Note SDN/24/03. https://www.imf.org/en/Publications/Staff-Discussion-Notes/AI-develo ping-economies

Katz, L. F., & Krueger, A. B. (2017). *The rise and nature of alternative work arrangements in the United States, 1995–2015* (NBER Working Paper No. 22667).

Kellogg, K. C., Valentine, M. A., & Christin, A. (2020). Algorithms at work: The new contested terrain of control. *Academy of Management Annals, 14*(1), 366–410. https://doi.org/10.5465/annals.2018.0174

Korinek, A., & Stiglitz, J. E. (2021). Artificial intelligence and its implications for income distribution and unemployment. NBER Working Paper No. 28436.

Lee, K. (2022). AI education and equity: Avoiding the automation divide. *Educational Policy, 36*(1), 157–181. https://doi.org/10.1177/089590482 11037845

Lee, M. K., Kusbit, D., Metsky, E., & Dabbish, L. (2019). Working with machines: The impact of algorithmic and data-driven management on human workers. In *Proceedings of the 33rd Annual ACM Conference on Human Factors in Computing Systems* (pp. 1603–1612). https://doi.org/10.1145/2702123.2702548

Li, K., Wang, Y., & Wang, Y. (2021). Artificial intelligence and economic growth: A comparative analysis of developing and developed economies. *Technological Forecasting and Social Change, 169*, Article 120793. https://doi.org/10.1016/j.techfore.2021.120793

LinkedIn Economic Graph. (2024). *Future of work report: AI skills and job market trends*. LinkedIn Corporation. https://economicgraph.linkedin.com/research/future-of-work-report-ai

Lomas, Natasha. (2023). "Google's AI-boosted search draws regulatory scrutiny. *TechCrunch*. https://techcrunch.com/2023/08/04/google-ai-search-eu-reg ulation.

Mazzucato, M. (2021). Mission economy: A moonshot guide to changing capitalism. *Harper Business*.

McKinsey Global Institute. (2024). *The future of work after COVID-19*. McKinsey & Company.

McCourt, W. (2024). *Digital infrastructure and public value: Reclaiming the platform state*. Oxford University Press.

Metz, Cade. (2023, January 23). "Microsoft Invests $10 Billion in OpenAI, extending partnership. *The New York Times*. https://www.nytimes.com/2023/01/23/technology/microsoft-invests-openai.html.

MIT Work of the Future Task Force. (2024). *Human-AI collaboration in the workplace: Performance outcomes and design principles*. Massachusetts Institute of Technology. https://workofthefuture.mit.edu/research/human-ai-collaboration

Mohieldin, Mahmoud, and Racha Ramadan. *Could Digital Inclusion Close the Gender Economic Gap in the MENA Region?* World Bank Policy Research Working Paper 10531, January 2024.

Morandini, M., et al. (2020). Social partnership and digital transformation: Lessons from Germany. *European Journal of Industrial Relations, 26*(3), 217–233. https://doi.org/10.1177/0959680120921432

Naudé, W. (2019). *The race against the robots and the fallacy of the giant cheesecake: Immediate and imagined impacts of artificial intelligence*. IZA Discussion Paper No. 12218.

Ndemo, B., & Weiss, T. (2017). *Digital Kenya: An entrepreneurial revolution in the making*. Palgrave Macmillan.

Ndung'u, N., & Signé, L. (2020). *The fourth industrial revolution and digitization will transform Africa into a global powerhouse*. Brookings Institution.

OECD. (2024). *Social protection responses to technological change*. OECD Publishing.

Oxford Martin School. (2024). *Technology at work v4.0: Navigating the new automation landscape*. Oxford University.

PwC. (2024). *Global AI impact index: Sectoral analysis and workforce implications*. PricewaterhouseCoopers.

Rahwan, I., Cebrian, M., Obradovich, N., Bongard, J., Bonnefon, J. F., Breazeal, C., Crandall, J. W., Christakis, N. A., Couzin, I. D., Jackson, M. O., Jennings, N. R., Kamar, E., Kloumann, I. M., Larochelle, H., Lazer, D., McElreath, R., Mislove, A., Parkes, D. C., Pentland, A. S., ... & Wellman, M. (2019). Machine behaviour. *Nature, 568*(7753), 477–486. https://doi.org/10.1038/s41586-019-1138-y

Rodrik, D. (2018). New technologies, global value chains, and developing economies. Pathways for Prosperity Commission Background Paper Series No. 1.

Rodrik, D. (2015). Premature deindustrialization. *Journal of Economic Growth, 21*(1), 1–33. https://doi.org/10.1007/s10887-015-9122-3

Schwellnus, C., Geva, A., Pak, M., & Veiel, R. (2019). *Gig economy platforms: Boon or bane? OECD Economics Department* (Working Papers No. 1550).

Standing, G. (2017). *Basic income: And how we can make it happen*. Pelican Books.

Susskind, R., & Susskind, D. (2015). *The future of the professions: How technology will transform the work of human experts*. Oxford University Press.

UNCTAD. (2023). Digital economy report: Value creation and capture - Implications for developing countries. United Nations Conference on Trade and Development.

UNESCO. (2024). *Reimagining education systems for the AI era: A global framework*. UNESCO Publishing.

World Bank. (2024). *World development report: The changing nature of work in the age of AI*. World Bank Publications.

World Economic Forum. (2024). *Future of jobs report*. WEF Publishing.

CHAPTER 7

AI and Sustainable Cities—Smart Urban Development for a Greener Future

Abstract The integration of Artificial Intelligence (AI) in urban environments offers transformative opportunities to enhance sustainability, resilience, and quality of life. This chapter provides a comprehensive examination of how AI technologies are revolutionizing urban planning, services, and infrastructure across diverse global contexts. Through rigorous analysis of empirical evidence and case studies from both developed and developing economies, we explore AI applications in energy management, transportation optimization, waste reduction, and climate resilience. The chapter also addresses critical ethical considerations, implementation challenges, and governance frameworks necessary for human-centered, sustainable urban AI deployment. By identifying key success factors and offering strategic recommendations, we provide actionable insights for policymakers, urban planners, and stakeholders seeking to leverage AI for more sustainable cities.

Keywords Smart cities · Urban sustainability · AI in urban planning · Smart infrastructure · Urban resilience · Human-centered design · Sustainable urban development

7.1   Introduction: The Urban Sustainability Challenge

Cities stand at the nexus of global sustainability challenges, housing over 56% of the world's population while generating more than 70% of global carbon emissions and consuming 75% of natural resources (UN-Habitat, 2024). With projections indicating that nearly 70% of humanity will live in urban areas by 2050, cities represent both the epicenter of sustainability challenges and the proving ground for innovative solutions.

Artificial Intelligence (AI) offers unprecedented capabilities to address urban sustainability through:

- **Real-time data integration** across previously siloed urban systems
- **Predictive analytics** enabling proactive rather than reactive management
- **Optimization algorithms** that maximize resource efficiency while enhancing service quality
- **Automated systems** that can respond to changing conditions without human intervention

However, the implementation of AI in urban contexts raises significant questions about equity, privacy, governance, and the human experience of city life. Sustainable urban AI requires balancing technological sophistication with human-centered design and inclusive governance.

This chapter examines AI applications across key urban domains, analyzing implementation approaches, outcomes, and lessons learned from diverse global contexts. By identifying critical success factors and addressing implementation challenges, we provide a framework for utilizing AI to create cities that are not merely "smart" but genuinely sustainable.

7.2   Conceptual Framework: AI-Enabled Sustainable Urbanism

Before examining specific applications, we establish a conceptual framework for understanding how AI can contribute to sustainable urban development.

7.2.1 Dimensions of Urban Sustainability

Sustainable cities must balance multiple imperatives:

- **Environmental sustainability**: Reducing resource consumption, emissions, and waste
- **Economic vitality**: Supporting productive and inclusive economic activity
- **Social equity**: Ensuring all residents have access to opportunities and services
- **Resilience**: Maintaining function despite acute shocks and chronic stresses

AI can contribute across these dimensions, but implementations must be evaluated against this comprehensive understanding of sustainability rather than narrow technological or economic metrics.

7.2.2 The Urban AI Stack

Urban AI implementations can be conceptualized as a layered system:

1. **Data collection layer**: Sensors, cameras, networked devices, and human inputs
2. **Data integration layer**: Systems that combine, clean, and standardize diverse data streams
3. **Analytics layer**: AI algorithms that process data to generate insights and predictions
4. **Decision support layer**: Tools that present information to human decision-makers
5. **Automation layer**: Systems that implement decisions without human intervention

The configuration of this "stack" has significant implications for governance, transparency, and human agency in urban environments.

7.2.3 Urban AI Maturity Model

Cities demonstrate varying levels of AI implementation maturity:

- **Level 1: Exploratory**—Isolated pilot projects without systematic coordination
- **Level 2: Operational**—Functional AI systems addressing specific domains
- **Level 3: Integrated**—Connected AI applications with data sharing across departments
- **Level 4: Comprehensive**—Citywide AI ecosystem with governance frameworks
- **Level 5: Adaptive**—Self-improving systems responsive to changing urban conditions

Research by the World Economic Forum (2024) indicates that 65% of cities globally remain at Levels 1–2, while only 8% have reached Level 4 or 5, underscoring the early stage of urban AI implementation.

7.3   AI Applications in Urban Energy Systems

Energy consumption represents one of the largest contributors to urban environmental footprints, making it a critical domain for sustainability interventions.

7.3.1   Smart Grids and Energy Distribution

AI enables more efficient, reliable, and sustainable urban energy systems:

- **Demand forecasting**: Machine learning models predict energy needs with 90–95% accuracy, compared to 75–80% with traditional methods, enabling better matching of supply and demand (IEEE, 2024).
- **Distributed resource integration**: AI orchestrates complex networks of renewable sources, storage, and traditional generation, increasing renewable integration capacity by 45–60% (International Energy Agency, 2024).
- **Fault detection and self-healing**: Predictive analytics identify potential failures before they occur, reducing outages by 35–40% in implemented locations (Electric Power Research Institute, 2024).

Case Study: Singapore's AI-Enhanced Grid Management

Singapore implemented an integrated AI system for grid management that incorporates:

- Machine learning for 15-minute-ahead load forecasting
- Automated voltage and frequency control
- Dynamic integration of solar resources despite cloud variability

Results include:

- 32% increase in renewable energy integration
- 47% reduction in grid stabilization costs
- 28% decrease in carbon intensity of electricity
- 99.98% reliability despite increasing climate volatility

The success of Singapore's implementation stemmed from comprehensive sensor deployment, high-quality data governance, and close collaboration between utilities, technology providers, and research institutions (Energy Market Authority of Singapore, 2024).

7.3.2   Building Energy Optimization

Buildings account for approximately 40% of urban energy consumption, providing significant opportunities for AI-driven efficiency:

- **Smart building management systems**: AI-controlled HVAC, lighting, and equipment reduce energy consumption by 20–35% while maintaining or improving occupant comfort (American Council for an Energy-Efficient Economy, 2024).
- **Occupancy pattern learning**: Adaptive algorithms that understand building usage patterns perform 15–25% better than rule-based systems.
- **Predictive maintenance**: AI identifies maintenance needs before failure, reducing energy waste from poorly functioning equipment by 10–15%.
- **Energy disaggregation**: Machine learning separates consumption by device type, enabling targeted efficiency interventions.

Case Study: AI-Optimized Municipal Buildings in Barcelona

Barcelona implemented an AI building management system across 294 municipal buildings that:

- Integrates data from 62,000+ sensors
- Uses reinforcement learning to continuously optimize operations
- Provides dashboards for facility managers and occupants
- Identifies anomalies and maintenance needs

Results after 36 months of operation:

- 28% average reduction in energy consumption
- €3.7 million annual cost savings
- 21,500 tons of CO_2 emissions avoided annually
- 94% satisfaction rating from building occupants and managers

The system's success is attributed to its user-centered design process, comprehensive training program for facility staff, and integration with the city's broader sustainability initiatives (Barcelona Digital City, 2024).

7.4   AI in Urban Mobility and Transportation

Transportation represents a critical sustainability challenge, affecting emissions, land use, economic opportunity, and quality of life.

7.4.1   Intelligent Traffic Management

AI enables unprecedented capabilities in traffic optimization:

- **Adaptive traffic signal control**: Machine learning algorithms adjust traffic lights based on real-time conditions, reducing travel times by 15–25% and emissions by 10–20% (U.S. Department of Transportation, 2024).
- **Predictive congestion management**: AI models forecast traffic patterns and trigger preventive measures, avoiding 30–40% of congestion events.

- **Dynamic curb management**: AI optimizes the allocation of curb space for various uses (deliveries, ridesharing, parking), improving efficiency by 25–35%.
- **Emergency vehicle prioritization**: Automated systems create "green waves" for emergency responses, reducing response times by 20–30%.

Technical Components:

- Computer vision for vehicle detection and classification
- Deep learning for traffic pattern prediction
- Reinforcement learning for signal optimization
- Connected vehicle data integration
- Digital twins for scenario testing

7.4.2   Public Transit Optimization

AI enhances public transportation effectiveness and efficiency:

- **Route and schedule optimization**: Machine learning analysis of travel patterns enables transit agencies to improve service by 15–20% without increasing fleet size.
- **Demand-responsive transit**: AI-powered dynamic routing adjusts to real-time demand, improving service in low-density areas.
- **Predictive maintenance**: Algorithms identify maintenance needs before failures occur, reducing breakdowns by 35–40% and extending vehicle lifespan.
- **Passenger flow management**: AI analysis optimizes station design and operations, reducing crowding and improving transfers.

Case Study: Seoul's Integrated Mobility Management

Seoul's Metropolitan Government implemented an AI-powered mobility management system that:

- Integrates data from public transit, traffic sensors, shared mobility services, and weather
- Provides real-time optimization across transportation modes
- Delivers personalized mobility recommendations to citizens
- Enables scenario planning for infrastructure investments

Results include:

- 15% reduction in average commute times
- 23% increase in public transit ridership
- 18% decrease in transportation-related emissions
- 34% reduction in traffic congestion during peak hours
- Greater mobility equity across socioeconomic groups

The system's effectiveness stems from its comprehensive data integration, user-friendly interfaces, and governance framework that balances automation with human oversight (Seoul Metropolitan Government, 2024).

7.4.3   Electrification and New Mobility Services

AI enables the transition to more sustainable urban mobility systems:

- **Electric vehicle charging infrastructure optimization**: Machine learning determines optimal charging locations and dynamically manages charging to balance grid load.
- **Shared mobility services**: AI orchestrates vehicle fleets to maximize utilization while minimizing empty miles.
- **Mobility-as-a-Service platforms**: Algorithms integrate multiple transportation modes for seamless journey planning.
- **Autonomous vehicle integration**: AI manages the introduction of autonomous vehicles to complement rather than compete with mass transit.

The implementation of these technologies is still emerging, but early results indicate potential for 30–45% reductions in urban transportation emissions when deployed comprehensively (International Transport Forum, 2024).

7.5   Smart Water and Waste Management

Urban resource cycles represent critical sustainability domains where AI can drive significant improvements.

7.5.1   Water System Optimization

AI applications in urban water systems address both scarcity and quality challenges:

- **Leak detection and prevention**: Machine learning identifies potential leaks by analyzing pressure and flow data, reducing water loss by 25–40% in implemented systems (American Water Works Association, 2024).
- **Demand forecasting**: AI models predict water demand patterns with 85–95% accuracy, enabling more efficient pumping and treatment scheduling.
- **Quality monitoring**: Real-time sensors combined with AI analytics detect contamination events hours or days earlier than traditional testing.
- **Flood prediction and management**: Machine learning models incorporate weather data, soil conditions, and infrastructure status to predict and mitigate urban flooding.

Case Study: AI Water Management in Chennai, India

Chennai implemented an integrated water management system that incorporates:

- IoT sensor networks across the water distribution system
- Machine learning for leak detection and water demand forecasting
- Automated pressure management
- Mobile alerts for consumers and maintenance teams

Results include:

- 32% reduction in non-revenue water loss

- 28% decrease in pumping energy consumption
- 45% faster response time to infrastructure failures
- Equitable water distribution during seasonal scarcity

This implementation demonstrates how AI can enhance water sustainability even in cities with infrastructure challenges and climate vulnerability (Chennai Smart City Ltd., 2024).

7.5.2 Waste Management and Circular Economy

AI enables more efficient waste management and supports circular economy approaches:

- **Smart waste collection**: Route optimization algorithms reduce collection vehicle miles by 20–30%, cutting fuel consumption and emissions
- **Waste sorting and recycling**: Computer vision systems identify recyclables with 85–95% accuracy, dramatically improving recovery rates
- **Predictive waste generation models**: Machine learning forecasts waste volumes by neighborhood, enabling proactive management
- **Circular resource marketplaces**: AI matches waste outputs from one entity with potential resource inputs for others

Case Study: Amsterdam's AI-Driven Circular Economy Initiative

Amsterdam's integrated approach uses AI to advance circular economy goals through:

- Smart bins that monitor fill levels and waste composition
- Computer vision for automated waste sorting
- Predictive maintenance for waste infrastructure
- Digital marketplace connecting waste generators with potential users

Outcomes include:

- 34% increase in recycling rates

- 28% reduction in waste management operational costs
- 42% decrease in landfill volumes
- Creation of 215 jobs in circular economy businesses
- Significant pollution reduction in canals and public spaces

The system demonstrates how AI can enhance traditional waste management while enabling new circular economy business models (City of Amsterdam, 2024).

7.6 Urban Climate Resilience and Environmental Quality

Climate change poses significant threats to urban areas through extreme weather, sea-level rise, and changing temperature patterns. AI provides powerful tools for both mitigation and adaptation.

7.6.1 Climate Risk Assessment and Planning

AI enhances urban climate resilience planning through:

- **High-resolution climate impact modelling**: Machine learning downscales global climate models to city-specific predictions with 3–5 times greater spatial precision.
- **Infrastructure vulnerability assessment**: AI analysis identifies structures and systems at highest risk from climate impacts.
- **Adaptation scenario planning**: Machine learning models evaluate the effectiveness of different adaptation strategies under various climate scenarios.
- **Natural capital optimization**: AI helps identify where green infrastructure will provide maximum cooling, stormwater management, and carbon sequestration benefits.

Technical Components:

- Deep learning for climate pattern analysis
- Computer vision for infrastructure assessment
- Agent-based modeling for scenario simulation
- Optimization algorithms for intervention planning

7.6.2   Environmental Monitoring and Management

AI enables more comprehensive environmental quality monitoring:

- **Air quality prediction**: Machine learning models forecast pollution levels 24–72 hours in advance with 80–90% accuracy, enabling preventive interventions.
- **Urban heat island mapping**: Thermal imagery combined with AI analysis identifies hotspots for targeted cooling interventions.
- **Ecosystem health assessment**: Computer vision monitors urban green spaces for stress indicators and invasive species.
- **Noise pollution management**: Acoustic monitoring with AI classification distinguishes harmful noise sources for targeted mitigation.

Case Study: Copenhagen's Climate Adaptation System

Copenhagen implemented an integrated climate resilience platform that:

- Combines climate projections with city-specific data
- Identifies critical intervention points for flood prevention
- Optimizes blue-green infrastructure investments
- Provides decision support for both long-term planning and emergency response

Results include:

- 45% reduction in flood damage during extreme weather events
- 37% decrease in urban heat island effect in targeted neighborhoods
- 28% improvement in stormwater management capacity
- Significant cost avoidance compared to traditional infrastructure approaches
- Enhanced biodiversity and public space quality as co-benefits

Copenhagen's system demonstrates how AI can help cities address immediate climate threats while creating long-term environmental benefits (City of Copenhagen, 2024).

7.7 ETHICAL AND SOCIAL DIMENSIONS OF URBAN AI

While AI offers significant sustainability benefits, its implementation in urban contexts raises important ethical and social considerations.

7.7.1 Privacy and Surveillance Concerns

The data collection necessary for smart city functionality creates tension with privacy rights:

- **Public space monitoring**: Camera networks and sensors may capture personal information without explicit consent.
- **Behavioral tracking**: Movement patterns and service usage data may reveal sensitive information about individuals.
- **Function creep**: Systems deployed for one purpose (e.g., traffic management) may later be used for surveillance.
- **Data security vulnerabilities**: Centralized data collection creates attractive targets for cyberattacks.

Ethical Approaches:

- Privacy-by-design principles in system architecture
- Data minimization and anonymization techniques
- Transparent policies on data collection, usage, and retention
- Independent oversight and regular privacy audits

7.7.2 Equity and Digital Divide Considerations

Smart city benefits may be unevenly distributed without explicit attention to equity:

- **Infrastructure gaps**: Sensors, connectivity, and services may be concentrated in wealthy areas, creating data inequities.
- **Digital access disparities**: Residents without smartphones or digital literacy may be excluded from AI-enhanced services.
- **Algorithmic bias**: Systems trained on historical data may perpetuate existing patterns of discrimination.

- **Technology-driven gentrification**: Smart city investments may accelerate displacement in vulnerable neighborhoods.

Equity-Enhancing Strategies:

- Equity impact assessments for all AI deployments
- Inclusive design approaches ensuring accessibility across digital skill levels
- Participatory processes involving marginalized communities
- Deliberate distribution of benefits to underserved neighborhoods

7.7.3   Human-AI Interaction in Urban Spaces

The introduction of AI systems changes how people experience and interact with urban environments:

- **Legibility and agency**: Citizens may not understand how AI systems are influencing their environment, reducing their sense of agency
- **Public space quality**: Technology infrastructure may detract from historical, cultural, or aesthetic values of urban spaces
- **Community dynamics**: Automated systems may reduce human interactions that traditionally build social capital
- **Technological dependency**: Over-reliance on AI systems may create vulnerabilities when technology fails

Human-Centered Approaches:

- Transparent communication about AI systems' presence and function
- Preserving human control over critical urban functions
- Designing technology to enhance rather than replace human interaction
- Maintaining analog alternatives for essential services

Case Study: Barcelona's Ethical Smart City Approach

Barcelona implemented a comprehensive ethical framework for urban AI that includes:

- A Chief Digital Officer with oversight of all smart city initiatives
- Public data commons with transparent governance
- Requirement for all AI systems to serve clear public benefit goals
- Ongoing participatory processes for technology decisions

This approach has resulted in:

- Higher public trust in smart city initiatives (75% approval rating)
- More equitable distribution of digital infrastructure across neighborhoods
- Successful deployment of privacy-preserving technologies
- Innovation ecosystem that aligns commercial interests with public values

Barcelona's experience demonstrates that ethical considerations need not impede technological advancement but can instead enhance its sustainability impact (Barcelona Digital City, 2024).

7.8 Implementation Frameworks for Sustainable Urban AI

Successful implementation of AI for urban sustainability requires comprehensive frameworks addressing governance, technology architecture, and change management.

7.8.1 Governance Frameworks

Effective urban AI governance typically includes:

- **Cross-departmental coordination structures**: Breaking silos between traditionally separate functions (transportation, energy, waste, etc.)
- **Public–private partnership models**: Frameworks for collaboration that protect public interests while leveraging private expertise

- **Regulatory approaches**: Rules governing data collection, algorithm transparency, and system performance
- **Citizen engagement mechanisms**: Structured processes for incorporating resident input throughout the AI lifecycle

Governance Best Practices:

- Clear roles and responsibilities across stakeholders
- Transparent decision-making processes
- Regular performance evaluation against sustainability metrics
- Mechanisms for addressing unintended consequences

7.8.2   Technical Architecture and Standards

Technical frameworks enabling sustainable urban AI include:

- **Open architecture approaches**: Non-proprietary systems that avoid vendor lock-in and enable innovation
- **Interoperability standards**: Protocols allowing different systems to communicate and share data
- **Edge-cloud balance**: Appropriate distribution of processing between local devices and centralized systems
- **Security frameworks**: Comprehensive approaches to cybersecurity and resilience

Technical Success Factors:

- Scalable designs that can grow with city needs
- Modular approaches allowing component updates
- Data quality assurance processes
- Resilient systems that maintain function during disruptions

7.8.3   Change Management and Capacity Building

Successful implementations address human and organizational factors:

- **Skills development programs**: Training for municipal staff, contractors, and stakeholders
- **Organizational adaptation**: Changes to workflows, job descriptions, and departmental structures
- **Knowledge management systems**: Platforms for documenting and sharing implementation lessons
- **Stakeholder engagement**: Ongoing communication with affected communities

Case Study: Helsinki's MyData Approach

Helsinki implemented a comprehensive framework for urban data governance that:

- Gives citizens control over their personal data across city services
- Provides open APIs for service innovation while protecting privacy
- Incorporates sustainability criteria into all AI deployments
- Includes ongoing educational programs for both staff and residents

Results include:

- Successful deployment of 45+ AI applications across city functions
- 85% citizen satisfaction with digital services
- Vibrant ecosystem of civic technology innovators
- Consistent alignment between technological and sustainability goals

Helsinki's approach demonstrates how governance frameworks can create conditions for both technological innovation and sustainability outcomes (City of Helsinki, 2024).

7.9 Comparative Analysis: Urban AI Implementation Across Global Contexts

Urban AI implementation occurs in vastly different contexts, with varying resources, existing infrastructure, and governance traditions. This section analyses implementation patterns across economic development levels.

7.9.1 Implementation in Advanced Economies

Cities in high-income countries typically demonstrate:

- **Resource advantages**: Substantial funding, existing digital infrastructure, and technical expertise
- **Integration challenges**: Complex legacy systems requiring modernization
- **Governance complexity**: Multiple stakeholders with established roles and regulatory frameworks
- **Incremental approach**: Building on existing digital foundations

Representative Case: Toronto's Quayside Project

Toronto's Quayside project illustrates both opportunities and challenges in advanced economies:

- Comprehensive sustainability objectives (climate-positive development)
- Sophisticated technology integration
- Extensive stakeholder involvement
- Significant privacy and governance debates

The project's evolution—from initial partnership with Sidewalk Labs to its current implementation—demonstrates how social and governance considerations can prove more challenging than technical aspects in advanced economies (Waterfront Toronto, 2024).

7.9.2 Implementation in Emerging Economies

Cities in middle-income countries often show:

- **Strategic leapfrogging**: Bypassing legacy technologies to implement cutting-edge solutions
- **Rapid scaling**: Quick transition from pilots to large-scale deployment
- **Pragmatic approaches**: Focus on high-impact applications addressing urgent challenges

- **Hybrid governance models**: Combining centralized direction with public–private partnerships

Representative Case: Medellín's Smart City Transformation

Medellín, Colombia transformed from a city plagued by violence to a smart city leader through:

- AI-enhanced public transportation connecting marginalized neighborhoods
- Integrated monitoring of landslide risks in informal settlements
- Digital public services accessible through community centers
- Strong alignment between technology and social equity goals

The city achieved significant sustainability gains while addressing social inclusion, demonstrating how emerging economies can align technological and social innovation (City of Medellín, 2024).

7.9.3   Implementation in Developing Economies

Cities in low-income countries typically demonstrate:

- **Resource constraints**: Limited funding, infrastructure, and technical expertise
- **Mobile-first approaches**: Leveraging widespread mobile phone adoption rather than fixed infrastructure
- **Focus on essential services**: Prioritizing applications with immediate impact on basic needs
- **International partnership models**: Collaboration with development agencies and technology providers

Representative Case: Kigali's Smart Utilities Initiative

Kigali, Rwanda implemented targeted AI applications focused on essential services:

- Smart water management reducing non-revenue water by 40%

- AI-optimized public transport routes improving efficiency by 35%
- Mobile-based waste collection coordination
- Solar-powered environmental monitoring network

Kigali's approach demonstrates how developing cities can achieve significant sustainability improvements through focused AI applications that address local priorities within resource constraints (City of Kigali, 2024).

7.9.4   Cross-Cutting Success Factors

Despite contextual differences, several success factors appear consistently across economic development levels:

- **Clear alignment with local priorities**: Successful implementations address specific challenges rather than pursuing technology for its own sake
- **Strong political leadership**: Executive champions who maintain focus on both technology and sustainability goals
- **Appropriate technology selection**: Solutions matched to infrastructure capabilities and maintenance capacity
- **Inclusive stakeholder engagement**: Meaningful participation by affected communities throughout planning and implementation
- **Skills development**: Investments in local capacity building to ensure long-term sustainability

Research by the World Bank (2024) indicates that urban AI implementations adhering to these principles are 3–4 times more likely to achieve sustained positive outcomes regardless of economic context.

7.10   STRATEGIC RECOMMENDATIONS FOR STAKEHOLDERS

Drawing on the evidence presented throughout this chapter, we offer strategic recommendations for key stakeholder groups.

7.10.1   Recommendations for Urban Policymakers and Leaders

- **Develop integrated AI strategies** that connect technological initiatives with sustainability goals
- **Establish robust governance frameworks** addressing privacy, equity, and transparency before implementing advanced systems
- **Prioritize open architectures and interoperability** to avoid vendor lock-in and enable innovation
- **Create dedicated capacity-building programs** to develop local expertise
- **Implement comprehensive performance monitoring** using sustainability metrics rather than purely technological measures

7.10.2   Recommendations for Technology Providers

- **Adopt human-centered design approaches that prioritize user needs and accessibility**
- **Develop solutions adaptable to different infrastructure contexts**
- **Embrace interoperability and open standards**
- **Incorporate equity considerations throughout the design process**
- **Build business models that align profit incentives with sustainability outcomes**

7.10.3   Recommendations for Civil Society Organizations

- **Develop expertise to participate meaningfully in urban AI governance**
- **Advocate for inclusive design and equitable deployment**
- **Monitor implementations for unintended consequences**
- **Facilitate community participation in technology planning and evaluation**
- **Build bridges between technical experts and community needs**

7.10.4   Implementation Roadmap

Urban stakeholders seeking to implement AI for sustainability should consider this phased approach:

1. **Assessment and Planning (3–6 months)**
   - Evaluate existing systems and infrastructure
   - Define priority sustainability challenges
   - Develop governance framework
   - Engage stakeholders in goal-setting
2. **Foundation Building (6–12 months)**
   - Establish data infrastructure
   - Implement privacy and security protocols
   - Develop performance metrics
   - Build skills and organizational capacity
3. **Initial Implementation (12–18 months)**
   - Deploy targeted pilots in high-priority domains
   - Evaluate technical performance and sustainability impacts
   - Refine approaches based on early results
   - Expand stakeholder engagement
4. **Scaling and Integration (18 + months)**
   - Expand successful pilots to full deployment
   - Integrate across previously separate domains
   - Develop advanced analytics capabilities
   - Implement continuous improvement processes

This phased approach allows cities to build necessary foundations while delivering early results, learning from implementation experience, and maintaining alignment with sustainability goals.

7.10.5   Conclusion

Artificial Intelligence offers transformative potential for urban sustainability, enabling cities to manage resources more efficiently, provide better services with fewer environmental impacts, and build resilience against growing climate threats. The evidence presented in this chapter demonstrates that AI can contribute significantly to sustainable urban development when implemented thoughtfully.

However, realizing this potential requires more than technological sophistication. Successful urban AI implementations demonstrate several critical characteristics:

1. **Clear purpose beyond technology**—Focusing on specific sustainability outcomes rather than AI deployment for its own sake
2. **Inclusive governance**—Ensuring diverse stakeholders participate meaningfully in planning and oversight
3. **Ethical frameworks**—Addressing privacy, equity, and transparency proactively rather than reactively
4. **Context-appropriate solutions**—Adapting approaches to local conditions, infrastructure, and capabilities
5. **Integration across domains**—Breaking down silos between traditional urban management sectors
6. **Human-centered design**—Enhancing rather than replacing human judgment and interaction

As cities continue to grow in both size and significance, their sustainability performance will increasingly determine global outcomes. AI provides powerful tools to improve this performance, but the technology alone is insufficient. By combining technological innovation with thoughtful governance, inclusive processes, and clear sustainability objectives, cities can leverage AI to create urban environments that are not just smart, but truly sustainable.

REFERENCES

American Council for an Energy-Efficient Economy. (2024). Smart buildings performance analysis: Energy savings and implementation strategies. ACEEE Research.
American Water Works Association. (2024). AI applications in urban water systems: Performance assessment. AWWA Research Foundation.
Barcelona Digital City. (2024). Ethical smart city framework: Implementation and outcomes. Barcelona City Council.
Chennai Smart City Ltd. (2024). Water management transformation through AI: Impact assessment. Government of Tamil Nadu.
City of Amsterdam. (2024). Circular economy initiative: Technology integration and outcomes. Amsterdam City Council.

City of Copenhagen. (2024). Climate adaptation system: Performance evaluation 2022–2024. Copenhagen Technical and Environmental Administration.

City of Helsinki. (2024). MyData approach: Governance and implementation report. Helsinki City Executive Office.

City of Kigali. (2024). Smart utilities initiative: Implementation review. City of Kigali.

City of Medellín. (2024). Smart city social transformation: Ten-year assessment. Medellín Mayor's Office.

Electric Power Research Institute. (2024). AI-enhanced grid reliability: Outage reduction analysis. EPRI Technical Report.

Energy Market Authority of Singapore. (2024). *AI in power grid management: Implementation case study.* Government of Singapore.

IEEE. (2024). AI applications in urban energy systems: Technical standards and performance metrics. IEEE Smart Cities Working Group.

International Energy Agency. (2024). *Smart energy systems for urban sustainability.* IEA Publications.

International Transport Forum. (2024). *New mobility technologies: Environmental impact assessment.* OECD Publications.

Seoul Metropolitan Government. (2024). Integrated mobility management system: Performance report. Seoul Smart City Office.

UN-Habitat. (2024). World cities report 2024: Urban resource consumption patterns. United Nations.

U.S. Department of Transportation. (2024). *Intelligent transportation systems: Performance metrics from urban deployments.* Federal Highway Administration.

Waterfront Toronto. (2024). *Quayside redevelopment: Technology and sustainability integration.* Waterfront Toronto.

World Bank. (2024). *Urban AI implementation: Comparative analysis across income levels.* World Bank Urban Development Series.

World Economic Forum. (2024). *Urban AI maturity model: Global assessment.* WEF Cities and Urbanization Platform.

CHAPTER 8

AI and Biodiversity—Protecting Nature Through Technology

Abstract Biodiversity loss represents one of humanity's most pressing environmental challenges, with potentially catastrophic consequences for ecosystem services, food security, and human well-being. This chapter examines how artificial intelligence (AI) can transform biodiversity conservation and ecosystem management through enhanced monitoring capabilities, predictive analytics, and decision support tools. Drawing on empirical evidence and case studies from terrestrial, marine, and freshwater contexts, we analyze AI applications in species identification, habitat monitoring, anti-poaching efforts, and climate resilience. The chapter addresses ethical considerations unique to conservation applications of AI, including data sovereignty, indigenous knowledge integration, and equity concerns. Through rigorous assessment of implementation challenges, success factors, and emerging approaches, we provide a comprehensive framework for leveraging AI technologies to protect biodiversity while ensuring these applications remain ethical, inclusive, and effective across diverse global contexts.

Keywords Biodiversity conservation · Ecosystem monitoring · Wildlife protection · Conservation technology · Environmental AI · Species identification · Habitat preservation · Conservation management

© The Author(s), under exclusive license to Springer Nature   153
Switzerland AG 2025
M. Mohieldin et al., *AI-Powered Sustainable Business*, Palgrave Studies
in Moral and Mindful Approaches to Leadership and Business,
https://doi.org/10.1007/978-3-031-93357-8_8

8.1 Introduction: Biodiversity in Crisis and the Promise of AI

The planet faces an unprecedented biodiversity crisis, with extinction rates estimated at 100–1,000 times historical baseline levels. According to the Intergovernmental Science-Policy Platform on Biodiversity and Ecosystem Services (IPBES, 2024), approximately one million species currently face extinction, representing a systemic collapse that threatens ecosystem services fundamental to human civilization. This crisis directly undermines progress toward multiple Sustainable Development Goals, including those related to food security, clean water, climate action, and economic development.

Traditional conservation approaches—while valuable—face significant limitations in scale, speed, and precision. Conservation managers typically work with limited data, constrained resources, and increasing threats, creating a critical need for more effective tools and methodologies. Artificial intelligence offers transformative potential by:

- **Expanding monitoring capacity**: Automating the collection and analysis of biodiversity data across vast areas
- **Revealing hidden patterns**: Identifying complex ecological relationships and threats invisible to human observers
- **Enabling prediction**: Forecasting changes and intervention outcomes with greater accuracy
- **Accelerating responses**: Reducing the time between threat detection and conservation action

However, realizing this potential requires navigating significant technical, ethical, and implementation challenges. Conservation contexts often feature limited infrastructure, sparse data, and complex stakeholder relationships that complicate technology deployment.

This chapter presents a comprehensive examination of AI's role in biodiversity conservation, analyzing current applications, implementation challenges, ethical considerations, and future opportunities. Through rigorous assessment of case studies and empirical evidence, we develop a framework for understanding how AI can enhance conservation effectiveness while ensuring applications remain ethical, inclusive, and appropriate for diverse ecological and social contexts.

8.2   Conceptual Framework: AI in the Conservation Cycle

Before examining specific applications, we establish a conceptual framework for understanding how AI integrates with the broader conservation management cycle.

8.2.1   The Conservation Management Cycle

Conservation typically follows an iterative cycle of:

1. **Assessment**: Measuring current biodiversity status and threats
2. **Planning**: Developing strategies and interventions
3. **Implementation**: Executing conservation actions
4. **Monitoring**: Tracking outcomes and impacts
5. **Adaptation**: Adjusting approaches based on results

AI can enhance each stage of this cycle, but applications must be strategically integrated rather than implemented as standalone technologies.

8.2.2   Conservation AI Technology Stack

Conservation AI implementations can be conceptualized as a layered system:

1. **Data acquisition layer:** Sensors, cameras, satellite imagery, and human observations
2. **Data management layer:** Systems for storing, organizing, and sharing biodiversity data
3. **Analytics layer:** Algorithms that process data to generate insights and predictions
4. **Decision support layer:** Tools that inform conservation planning and management
5. **Intervention layer:** Systems that implement or support conservation actions

The configuration of this stack has significant implications for effectiveness, access, and sustainability of conservation technology.

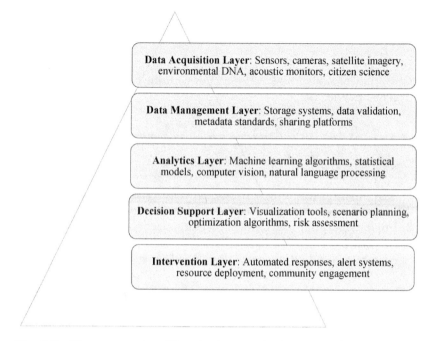

Fig. 8.1 The conservation AI technology stack. *Source* Developed based on analysis of conservation technology implementations described in this chapter

Figure 8.1 illustrates the layered structure of conservation AI systems. This conceptual framework helps organizations understand the components required for effective implementation and identify where their current capabilities may need strengthening.

8.2.3   Conservation AI Readiness Framework

Organizations and regions demonstrate varying capacity for implementing AI conservation tools. This capacity can be assessed across multiple dimensions:

- **Data readiness**: Availability of baseline biodiversity data, monitoring systems, and data management infrastructure

- **Technical infrastructure**: Access to computing resources, connectivity, and supporting technologies
- **Human capacity**: Skills in data science, ecology, and technology management
- **Governance frameworks**: Policies for data sharing, algorithm transparency, and decision authority
- **Financial sustainability**: Resources for both implementation and long-term maintenance

Understanding these capacity dimensions is essential for designing appropriate conservation AI applications and implementation strategies.

8.3   AI Applications in Biodiversity Monitoring

Effective conservation requires a comprehensive understanding of species distributions, population trends, and ecosystem health. AI dramatically enhances monitoring capabilities through automated data collection and analysis.

8.3.1   Automated Species Identification and Counting

Machine learning has revolutionized the identification of species in images, audio, and other data types:

- **Camera trap image processing**: Computer vision algorithms now identify species in camera trap images with 95%+ accuracy for many taxonomic groups, reducing human processing time by up to 99% (Conservation AI Lab, 2024).
- **Acoustic monitoring**: Machine learning identifies bird, amphibian, and mammal vocalizations in audio recordings with 85–98% accuracy, enabling continuous monitoring across vast areas.
- **Drone and aerial imagery analysis**: AI algorithms detect and count animals in aerial imagery with 90%+ accuracy for large-bodied species, enabling broader and more frequent surveys.
- **Citizen science data verification**: Machine learning validates species identifications from community scientists, improving data quality while expanding collection capacity.

These technologies enable biodiversity monitoring at unprecedented scales. For example, the Wildlife Insights platform processes over 20 million camera trap images annually across 45 countries, providing data on more than 1,200 species with minimal human review (Wildlife Conservation Society, 2024).

Technical Components:

- Convolutional neural networks for image classification
- Recurrent neural networks for bioacoustics analysis
- Transfer learning to adapt models across species and contexts
- Edge computing for deployment in remote environments

Table 8.1 compares the performance of AI across different data types used for species identification. This comparison highlights both the significant advances in automated identification and the varying effectiveness across different taxonomic groups and data collection methods.

8.3.2   Remote Sensing for Ecosystem Monitoring

AI transforms satellite and airborne data into actionable conservation intelligence:

- **Habitat classification and mapping**: Deep learning models distinguish 30+ habitat types with 85–95% accuracy, enabling detailed ecosystem mapping at landscape scales
- **Deforestation detection**: Machine learning algorithms detect forest loss within days rather than months, with alerts generated for areas as small as 0.1 hectares
- **Ecosystem health assessment**: AI models analyze spectral signatures to assess vegetation condition, disease presence, and invasive species
- **Land use change monitoring**: Algorithms track conversion of natural habitats to agricultural or urban land with 90%+ accuracy

Case Study: Global Forest Watch

The Global Forest Watch platform demonstrates the transformative potential of AI for forest monitoring:

Table 8.1 AI applications in species identification across data types

Data type	Current accuracy range (%)	Processing efficiency gain	Most effective for	Key limitations	Notable implementation example
Camera trap images	85–97	99% reduction in human processing time	Medium to large mammals, birds	Lower accuracy for similar species, juvenile identification	Wildlife Insights platform: 20+ million images processed annually across 45 countries
Acoustic recordings	80–95	90% reduction in analysis time	Birds, bats, cetaceans, amphibians, insects	Background noise sensitivity, overlapping calls	Rainforest Connection: 20+ threatened species monitored across 22 countries
Aerial/drone imagery	85–96	75% reduction in survey costs	Large-bodied animals, herd species	Limited to visible animals, canopy penetration issues	Great Elephant Census: 350,000+ elephants counted across 18 countries
Environmental DNA	70–85	60% reduction in laboratory time	Fish, amphibians, invertebrates	Taxonomic database limitations, contamination sensitivity	eBioAtlas: mapping freshwater biodiversity across 30 countries
Citizen science photos	75–90	80% reduction in expert validation time	Distinctive plants, insects, birds	Variable image quality, sampling bias	iNaturalist: 500+ million observations, 70,000+ species identified

Source Compiled from Conservation AI Lab (2024), Wildlife Conservation Society (2024), and additional sources cited in this chapter

- Uses machine learning to analyze petabytes of satellite imagery
- Provides near-real-time deforestation alerts across the tropics
- Enables customized monitoring of specific conservation areas
- Supports enforcement, certification, and policy applications

Results include:

- 273 million hectares of forest under improved monitoring
- 45% reduction in response time to illegal clearing in monitored areas
- 23% decrease in deforestation in areas with active monitoring programs
- Support for indigenous land defenders across 15+ countries

The system's success stems from combining sophisticated AI with accessible interfaces, allowing users ranging from government agencies to local communities to leverage powerful analytics without specialized technical expertise (World Resources Institute, 2024).

8.3.3   Integrated Biodiversity Monitoring Systems

The most advanced applications combine multiple AI approaches for comprehensive ecosystem understanding:

- **Multi-sensor integration**: Combining satellite imagery, ground sensors, camera traps, and acoustic monitors for holistic ecosystem monitoring
- **Species-habitat relationship modeling**: AI algorithms that correlate species occurrences with environmental variables to predict distributions across unsampled areas
- **Automated change detection**: Systems that identify significant ecological changes and trigger appropriate responses
- **Digital twins for ecosystems**: Integrating multiple data streams into simulation models that predict ecosystem responses

Case Study: Amazon Basin Monitoring System

An international consortium implemented an integrated monitoring system for the Amazon basin that incorporates:

- Satellite monitoring with AI-based deforestation detection
- Camera trap networks with automated species identification
- Acoustic sensors for biodiversity assessment
- Community reporting through mobile applications
- Integration of indigenous knowledge through participatory mapping

This system provides unprecedented visibility into Amazonian ecosystems, enabling:

- 40% faster detection of environmental threats
- 35% improvement in enforcement effectiveness
- First basin-wide biodiversity indicators with monthly updates
- Documentation of previously unrecorded species distributions
- Empowerment of indigenous communities as conservation partners

The system demonstrates how multiple AI applications can be integrated to create monitoring capabilities far beyond what any single technology could provide (Amazon Conservation Team, 2024).

The adoption of AI-enhanced monitoring varies significantly across regions, reflecting differences in conservation priorities, infrastructure, and resources. Figure 8.2 illustrates the global distribution of major AI monitoring implementations, highlighting both innovation hotspots and critical gaps in coverage.

8.4   AI in Combating Wildlife Crime

Wildlife crime—including poaching and illegal wildlife trade—represents a major driver of biodiversity loss, with an estimated annual value exceeding $20 billion (UNEP, 2024). AI provides powerful tools for detecting, preventing, and responding to these threats.

8.4.1   Predictive Analytics for Poaching Prevention

AI enables transition from reactive to proactive anti-poaching approaches:

- **Poaching risk prediction**: Machine learning models analyze historical incident data, weather patterns, animal movements, and other variables to predict high-risk areas and times with 75–85% accuracy.
- **Patrol route optimization**: AI algorithms generate patrol routes that maximize coverage of high-risk areas while considering terrain, resource constraints, and past patrol effectiveness.
- **Anomaly detection**: Systems identify unusual patterns in animal movements or other indicators that may signal poaching activity.

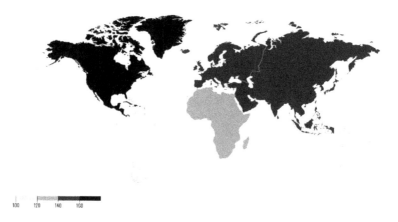

Region	Active AI Monitoring Projects	Species Coverage	Primary Applications
North America	175+	2,400+ species	Wildlife management, habitat protection
Africa	120+	1,800+ species	Anti-poaching, protected area monitoring
Asia	150+	2,100+ species	Tiger conservation, forest protection
Latin America	95+	3,200+ species	Deforestation monitoring, biodiversity surveys
Europe	140+	1,600+ species	Habitat directive compliance, restoration monitoring
Oceania	85+	1,300+ species	Invasive species detection, reef monitoring

Fig. 8.2 Global distribution of AI-enhanced biodiversity monitoring systems. *Source* Compiled from multiple sources including Conservation AI Lab (2024), Wildlife Conservation Society (2024), and World Resources Institute (2024). Image by ultimaps.com

- **Behavioral analysis**: Machine learning identifies patterns in poacher behavior to anticipate tactics and preferred targets.

Technical Components:

- Ensemble methods combining multiple prediction models
- Geospatial analysis with machine learning enhancement
- Reinforcement learning for patrol optimization
- Bayesian networks for threat assessment

8.4.2 Surveillance and Early Warning Systems

AI enhances detection capabilities across protected areas:

- **Smart camera networks**: Computer vision systems automatically analyze footage to detect humans, vehicles, or weapons in protected areas, generating real-time alerts.
- **Acoustic monitoring**: AI analysis of sound data identifies gunshots, vehicle movements, or other human activity signatures.
- **Thermal imaging analysis**: Machine learning detects humans in thermal imagery with 90%+ accuracy, enabling nighttime surveillance.
- **Integrated early warning networks**: Systems that combine multiple detection technologies with automated alert distribution.

Case Study: PAWS (Protection Assistant for Wildlife Security)

The PAWS system demonstrates the effectiveness of AI for anti-poaching:

- Uses machine learning to predict poaching risk based on historical patterns
- Generates optimized patrol routes considering terrain and resource constraints
- Continuously improves through feedback from patrol results
- Integrates with existing conservation management software

Implementation across three wildlife reserves in Southeast Asia resulted in:

- 35% increase in detection of poaching activities
- 60% reduction in snares and traps within protected areas
- More efficient use of limited ranger resources
- Evidence-based adaptation of protection strategies

PAWS demonstrates how AI can amplify the effectiveness of traditional conservation resources through more strategic deployment (Harvard Centre for Research in Computation and Society, 2024).

8.4.3   *Disrupting Wildlife Trafficking Networks*

AI helps combat wildlife crime beyond protected area boundaries:

- **Online wildlife trafficking detection**: Natural language processing and image recognition identify wildlife products in e-commerce platforms and social media with 85% + accuracy.
- **Transportation screening**: Computer vision systems detect wildlife products in luggage, cargo, and mail with significantly higher accuracy than manual inspection.
- **Financial pattern recognition**: Machine learning identifies suspicious transaction patterns associated with wildlife trafficking.
- **Network analysis**: AI systems map trafficking networks by analyzing communications, transactions, and transportation patterns.

Technical Components:

- Natural language processing for text analysis
- Computer vision for product identification
- Anomaly detection for financial monitoring
- Network analysis algorithms for criminal organization mapping

These technologies enable more effective intervention throughout wildlife trafficking supply chains, complementing protected area enforcement efforts.

8.5   AI FOR SPECIES AND ECOSYSTEM CONSERVATION PLANNING

Beyond monitoring and enforcement, AI enhances conservation planning through improved analysis, prediction, and optimization.

8.5.1   *Species Distribution and Population Modelling*

AI provides unprecedented ability to understand and predict species distributions:

- **Species distribution models**: Machine learning approaches outperform traditional statistical methods by 15–40% in predicting species occurrences across landscapes.
- **Population viability analysis**: AI models incorporate more complex variables to better predict population trajectories under different scenarios.
- **Connectivity modeling**: Network analysis algorithms identify critical movement corridors and habitat linkages for conservation prioritization.
- **Genetic diversity mapping**: Machine learning combines genetic, environmental, and occurrence data to map genetic diversity patterns crucial for conservation planning.

Technical Applications:

- Ensemble modeling approaches combining multiple algorithms
- Deep learning for complex pattern recognition
- Bayesian networks for uncertainty quantification
- Agent-based models for population dynamics

8.5.2 Protected Area Planning and Management

AI enhances the design and management of conservation areas:

- **Systematic conservation planning**: AI optimization algorithms identify protected area configurations that maximize biodiversity representation while considering implementation constraints.
- **Management effectiveness prediction**: Machine learning models predict conservation outcomes from different management approaches, enabling more effective intervention design.
- **Visitor impact management**: AI analysis optimizes tourism and recreation to minimize ecological impacts while maintaining visitor experiences.
- **Resource allocation optimization**: Algorithms determine the most efficient distribution of limited conservation resources across protected area networks.

Case Study: Madagascar Conservation Planning

Conservation International implemented an AI-enhanced planning system for Madagascar's protected area network:

- Used machine learning to model distributions of 2,300 + endemic species
- Employed optimization algorithms to identify priority conservation areas
- Incorporated climate change projections to ensure long-term effectiveness
- Integrated socioeconomic factors affecting implementation feasibility

Results included:

- Protected area design capturing 95% of endemic species with 28% less area than previous approaches
- 40% improvement in climate resilience of conservation network
- 35% reduction in potential social conflicts through improved planning
- Successful implementation of new protected areas covering 570,000 hectares

This implementation demonstrates how AI can enhance conservation planning by handling complexity beyond human analytical capacity while incorporating both ecological and social factors (Conservation International, 2024).

8.5.3   *Ecosystem Restoration and Rehabilitation*

AI supports the growing field of ecological restoration:

- **Restoration site prioritization**: Machine learning identifies areas where restoration will provide maximum ecological return on investment.
- **Intervention optimization**: AI models predict outcomes of different restoration techniques to guide methodology selection.

- **Progress monitoring**: Computer vision tracks vegetation recovery and ecosystem development through satellite or drone imagery.
- **Adaptive management**: Systems continuously update restoration approaches based on monitoring feedback.

Technical Components:

- Multi-criteria decision analysis with machine learning
- Ecosystem modeling using neural networks
- Computer vision for vegetation analysis
- Bayesian optimization for adaptive management

These applications enhance restoration outcomes while reducing costs through more precise intervention and monitoring.

8.6 AI FOR CLIMATE RESILIENCE IN BIODIVERSITY CONSERVATION

Climate change represents an existential threat to biodiversity, requiring conservation approaches that anticipate and adapt to changing conditions.

8.6.1 Climate Impact Prediction for Species and Ecosystems

AI enhances understanding of climate vulnerability:

- **Climate-driven range shift prediction**: Machine learning models predict species range changes under climate scenarios with 30–50% greater accuracy than traditional approaches.
- **Vulnerability assessment**: AI algorithms identify species and ecosystems most at risk from climate impacts based on traits and exposure.
- **Tipping point identification**: Machine learning detects early warning signals of potential ecosystem transformations.
- **Interaction network analysis**: AI models examine how climate disruptions to one species may cascade through ecological networks.

Technical Components:

- Ensemble forecasting integrating multiple models

- Deep learning for pattern recognition in climate-biodiversity relationships
- Network analysis of species interactions
- Time series analysis for trend detection

8.6.2   Climate-Smart Conservation Strategies

AI supports development of conservation approaches robust to climate change:

- **Climate-resilient protected area design**: Algorithms identify conservation networks that maintain effectiveness under changing conditions.
- **Connectivity planning for climate adaptation**: Machine learning identifies corridors that will facilitate climate-driven migrations.
- **Assisted migration decision support**: AI systems help evaluate when and where managed relocation of species may be necessary.
- **Ex-situ conservation prioritization**: Models identify species requiring captive breeding or seed banking due to climate vulnerability.

Case Study: Great Barrier Reef Climate Resilience Program

The Great Barrier Reef Marine Park Authority implemented an AI-driven resilience system:

- Uses machine learning to predict coral bleaching events 2–3 weeks in advance
- Identifies reef areas with highest recovery potential
- Optimizes intervention deployment during heat stress events
- Guides long-term coral reef restoration efforts

Results include:

- 28% reduction in coral mortality during heat stress events

- 45% improvement in intervention efficiency through targeted deployment
- 35% increase in coral recruitment in actively managed areas
- More effective engagement of tourism operators in reef protection

The system demonstrates how AI can help manage complex climate impacts on sensitive ecosystems by providing timely information, optimizing limited resources, and supporting evidence-based decision-making (Great Barrier Reef Foundation, 2024).

Table 8.2 summarizes key technical approaches to integrating climate considerations into conservation planning through AI. This overview highlights how different algorithms and data sources can be combined to address the complex challenge of protecting biodiversity under changing climate conditions.

8.7 ETHICAL CONSIDERATIONS IN CONSERVATION AI

The application of AI in biodiversity conservation raises unique ethical questions that must be addressed for both moral and practical reasons.

8.7.1 Data Sovereignty and Ownership

Questions about who controls and benefits from biodiversity data are increasingly significant:

- **Indigenous data sovereignty**: Many biodiversity hotspots are within indigenous territories, raising questions about rights to data collected in these areas.
- **National sovereignty concerns**: Countries increasingly assert rights over biodiversity data collected within their borders.
- **Commercial exploitation risks**: Valuable conservation data may be used for commercial purposes without equitable benefit sharing.
- **Knowledge commons approaches**: Developing models for shared governance of biodiversity data while respecting rights.

Ethical Approaches:

- Free, prior, and informed consent for data collection

Table 8.2 Technical approaches for climate-smart conservation using AI

Technical approach	Primary algorithms	Key data inputs	Conservation applications	Implementation challenges	Success metrics
Climate-niche modeling	Ensemble species distribution models, deep neural networks	Species occurrence records, climate variables, remote sensing data	Identifying future suitable habitats, planning protected area networks	Uncertainty in climate projections, limited occurrence data for rare species	Improved prediction accuracy (30–50% over traditional methods), better policy alignment
Connectivity analysis	Network theory algorithms, least-cost path analysis, circuit theory	Landscape features, species movement data, genetic relationships	Designing wildlife corridors, identifying critical connectivity nodes	Validating movement predictions, incorporating infrastructure barriers	Increased genetic exchange, documented species movements through corridors
Ecosystem transformation forecasting	Random forests, recurrent neural networks, Bayesian networks	Long-term monitoring data, remote sensing time series, soil condition	Early warning systems for ecosystem shifts, identifying intervention opportunities	Complex ecological interactions, non-linear response patterns	Lead time for intervention, reduction in ecosystem collapse events
Assisted migration planning	Multi-criteria decision analysis, genetic algorithms	Species traits, climate vulnerability assessments, habitat suitability	Evaluating translocation candidates, identifying recipient sites	Ethical considerations, ecological impact uncertainties	Establishment success rates, maintained genetic diversity
Ex-situ prioritization	Portfolio optimization algorithms, decision trees	Phylogenetic data, climate vulnerability, facility capacity	Seed banking prioritization, captive breeding program design	Resource constraints, incomplete trait data	Preserved genetic diversity, successful reintroductions

Source Compiled from multiple sources including Great Barrier Reef Foundation (2024) and additional literature cited in this chapter

- Benefit-sharing agreements for data utilization
- Community protocols for data governance
- Recognition of multiple knowledge systems and ownership models

Ethical implementation of conservation AI requires balancing multiple considerations across different dimensions. The Fig. 8.3 presents a framework for assessing ethical implications of conservation technology, highlighting the interconnected nature of these considerations and their relationship to both conservation and social outcomes.

8.7.2   Surveillance and Privacy Implications

Conservation monitoring technologies can impact human privacy and rights:

- **Human identification in protected areas**: Camera systems designed for wildlife may capture images of people without consent.
- **Indigenous and local community impacts**: Surveillance technologies may affect traditional practices in or near protected areas.
- **Dual-use concerns**: Technologies deployed for conservation may be repurposed for security or social control.
- **Proportionality questions**: Balancing legitimate conservation needs with privacy and autonomy rights.

Ethical Safeguards:

- Privacy-by-design approaches in technology development
- Clear policies on incidental human data collection
- Community consultation in surveillance technology deployment
- Independent oversight of monitoring systems

8.7.3   Traditional Knowledge Integration

Conservation AI must navigate the relationship with indigenous and local knowledge systems:

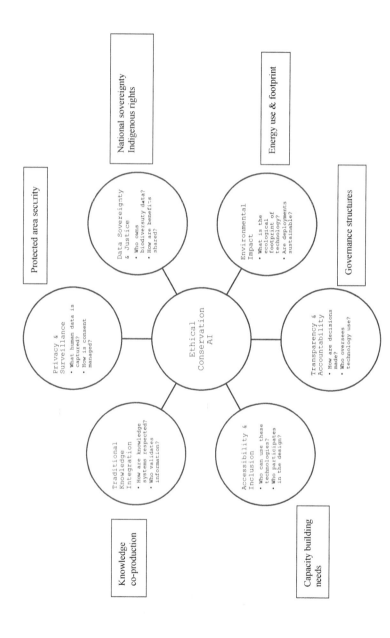

Fig. 8.3 Ethical considerations in conservation AI implementation. *Source* Developed based on analysis of case studies including Māori Biodiversity Monitoring (Toi Taiao Māori Biosecurity Network, 2024) and literature on conservation ethics

- **Knowledge validation concerns**: AI systems may be perceived as "validating" traditional knowledge rather than recognizing its inherent value.
- **Extraction without recognition**: Traditional knowledge may inform AI systems without appropriate acknowledgment or compensation.
- **Complementary knowledge systems**: Developing approaches that respect both scientific and traditional knowledge.
- **Power dynamics in knowledge production**: Addressing imbalances in who defines conservation priorities and approaches.

Inclusive Approaches:

- Co-design of conservation technology with knowledge holders
- Recognition of multiple ways of knowing in decision systems
- Compensation for knowledge contributions
- Governance frameworks that share decision authority

Case Study: Māori Biodiversity Monitoring in New Zealand

A collaboration between Māori communities and conservation technologists demonstrates ethical practice:

- Co-designed monitoring systems incorporating both AI and traditional indicators
- Developed community-controlled data governance
- Created interfaces that preserve cultural context of observations
- Established benefit-sharing for commercial applications

This approach resulted in:

- More comprehensive biodiversity monitoring covering both scientific and cultural indicators
- Higher community engagement in conservation efforts
- Protection of sensitive cultural knowledge while enabling collaboration

- More effective conservation outcomes through integrated approaches

The project shows how conservation AI can respect indigenous rights and knowledge while creating more effective conservation solutions through complementary approaches (Toi Taiao Māori Biosecurity Network, 2024).

8.8   IMPLEMENTATION CHALLENGES AND PRACTICAL CONSIDERATIONS

Beyond ethical questions, conservation AI implementation faces practical challenges that must be addressed for effective deployment.

8.8.1   Technical Infrastructure Limitations

Conservation often occurs in areas with significant infrastructure constraints:

- **Connectivity challenges**: Many biodiversity hotspots lack reliable internet access
- **Energy limitations**: Remote areas may have limited or unreliable power sources
- **Hardware durability issues**: Field conditions present challenges for electronic equipment
- **Maintenance complexity**: Technical support may be unavailable in remote locations

Adaptation Strategies:

- Edge computing solutions that operate without continuous connectivity
- Low-power system designs with solar or other renewable sources
- Ruggedized hardware designed for field conditions
- Simplified maintenance procedures and modular designs

8.8.2 Data Limitations and Biases

Conservation data present unique challenges for AI applications:

- **Data scarcity**: Many species and ecosystems lack sufficient data for traditional machine learning approaches
- **Sampling biases**: Existing data often reflect accessibility rather than ecological importance
- **Taxonomic biases**: Data availability varies dramatically across species groups
- **Temporal limitations**: Limited historical data complicate trend analysis

Technical Approaches:

- Few-shot learning methods that perform well with limited training data
- Transfer learning from data-rich to data-poor contexts
- Active learning systems that prioritize new data collection
- Explicit bias correction in model development

8.8.3 Capacity and Expertise Gaps

The intersection of conservation and AI creates significant human capacity challenges:

- **Interdisciplinary expertise scarcity**: Few individuals have both ecological knowledge and AI skills.
- **Technology adoption barriers**: Conservation organizations may lack experience with advanced technologies.
- **Maintenance and support limitations**: Technical capacity for ongoing support may be unavailable.
- **Knowledge transfer challenges**: Ensuring conservation practitioners can effectively use AI tools.

Capacity-Building Approaches:

- Targeted training programs bridging conservation and data science

- User-centered design focused on accessibility for non-technical users
- Remote support models connecting field implementations with technical expertise
- Peer learning networks sharing implementation experiences

Case Study: SMART Conservation Software

The Spatial Monitoring and Reporting Tool (SMART) demonstrates effective capacity building:

- Designed specifically for protected area management in challenging contexts
- Incorporates increasingly sophisticated AI components within an accessible interface
- Provides comprehensive training programs from basic to advanced levels
- Maintains a global support network with regional expertise

SMART's approach has enabled:

- Adoption by 3,000+ protected areas across 100 + countries
- Successful implementation in highly diverse technical contexts
- Sustained usage beyond initial project periods
- Progressive adoption of more advanced features as capacity develops

The platform demonstrates how conservation technology can be designed for accessibility while still incorporating sophisticated capabilities through thoughtful interface design and tiered learning approaches (SMART Conservation Partnership, 2024).

Table 8.3 provides a practical assessment framework for organizations considering conservation AI implementation. This matrix helps identify strengths and gaps across critical dimensions, enabling more strategic planning and resource allocation.

Table 8.3 Implementation readiness assessment framework for conservation AI

Readiness dimension	Basic readiness	Intermediate readiness	Advanced readiness	Assessment questions
Data assets	Limited historical data, primarily qualitative	Regular monitoring data with consistent methodology	Comprehensive baseline data with standardized collection protocols	What biodiversity data do we currently collect? How structured and accessible is it?
Technical infrastructure	Intermittent connectivity, limited computing resources	Reliable connectivity at headquarters, basic field equipment	Robust connectivity network, specialized conservation technology	What connectivity exists in implementation areas? What hardware is already deployed?
Human capacity	Basic digital literacy, limited technical staff	Dedicated technology roles, some data science expertise	Specialized conservation technology team, data science integration	What technology skills exist in the organization? What training would be needed?
Organizational processes	Ad hoc technology adoption, limited integration	Technology strategy exists, some integration with operations	Systematic approach to technology, data-driven decision making	How are technology decisions currently made? How is effectiveness evaluated?
Partnerships & support	Limited external technology relationships	Active partnerships with technology providers	Integrated partnership network including research institutions	What technology partnerships exist? What additional support would be needed?
Funding sustainability	Project-based technology funding	Multi-year technology budget	Long-term technology program with diverse funding	How would implementation and maintenance be funded? What is the sustainability model?

Source Derived from implementation experiences documented by SMART Conservation Partnership (2024) and other cases discussed in this chapter

8.9   FUTURE DIRECTIONS AND EMERGING APPROACHES

Conservation AI continues to evolve rapidly, with several promising directions for future development.

8.9.1   *Integrated Sentinels for Planetary Health*

Emerging systems combine biodiversity monitoring with broader planetary health indicators:

- **Multi-domain environmental monitoring**: Integrating biodiversity, climate, pollution, and other data streams
- **Early warning systems for ecosystem change**: AI powered detection of ecological shifts before they become obvious
- **Planetary boundaries monitoring**: Real-time tracking of key earth system processes
- **Cross-scale integration**: Connecting local observations to global patterns

These approaches promise more holistic understanding of biodiversity in its broader environmental context.

8.9.2   *Democratized Conservation Technology*

New approaches are making conservation AI more accessible to diverse users:

- **Low-cost hardware platforms:** Purpose-built devices bringing advanced capabilities at prices affordable for wider implementation
- **AutoML for conservation:** Systems that automate model development for users without data science expertise
- **Open source conservation tools:** Community-maintained software reducing financial barriers to adoption
- **Mobile-first platforms:** Conservation technologies designed primarily for smartphone access

These developments expand the potential user base for conservation AI beyond well-resourced organizations to include local conservation groups, indigenous communities, and citizen scientists.

8.9.3   Human-AI Collaborative Conservation

Evolving approaches emphasize complementary roles for human and artificial intelligence:

- **Human-in-the-loop systems**: Conservation tools that combine AI analysis with human judgment
- **Augmented intelligence approaches**: Technologies designed to enhance rather than replace human capabilities
- **Knowledge co-production**: Systems integrating scientific, traditional, and machine-generated knowledge
- **Adaptive management platforms**: Tools supporting continuous learning by both human users and AI systems

These collaborative approaches recognize that effective conservation requires both computational power and human wisdom, seeking to combine them in ways that leverage the strengths of each.

Case Study: Indigenous Guardians Program

A collaboration between indigenous communities and conservation technologists demonstrates emerging approaches:

- Developed easy-to-use mobile tools for biodiversity monitoring
- Created custom AI models trained on locally important species
- Integrated traditional knowledge indicators with scientific metrics
- Established community ownership of both data and technology

Results include:

- Monitoring coverage of 18 million hectares of traditional territories
- Documentation of 200+ species previously unrecorded in scientific literature
- Successful defense of land rights through evidence-based advocacy
- New conservation management approaches combining traditional and scientific knowledge

This initiative illustrates how conservation AI can be democratized and integrated with indigenous stewardship to create more effective and equitable approaches to biodiversity protection (Indigenous Guardians Toolkit, 2024).

8.10   STRATEGIC RECOMMENDATIONS FOR STAKEHOLDERS

Based on the evidence presented throughout this chapter, we offer strategic recommendations for key stakeholder groups.

8.10.1   Recommendations for Conservation Organizations

- Develop AI strategies aligned with conservation missions
- Invest in data infrastructure as foundation for AI applications
- Build internal capacity while leveraging external partnerships
- Implement ethical frameworks for technology deployment
- Share learnings through collaborative networks

8.10.2   Recommendations for Technology Developers

- Design for challenging implementation contexts
- Prioritize user needs over technical sophistication
- Address data limitations through appropriate methodologies
- Develop solutions complementary to human expertise
- Incorporate ethical considerations throughout development process

8.10.3   Recommendations for Funders and Policymakers

- Support development of conservation data infrastructure
- Fund capacity building alongside technology deployment
- Develop appropriate governance frameworks for conservation AI
- Promote open approaches that prevent monopolization
- Invest in long-term sustainability of conservation technology

8.10.4   Implementation Framework

Organizations seeking to implement conservation AI should consider this phased approach:

1. **Foundation Building (3–6 months)**
   - Assess existing data assets and gaps
   - Develop data management infrastructure
   - Establish ethical guidelines
   - Build initial technical capacity
2. **Initial Implementation (6–12 months)**
   - Deploy targeted applications addressing priority needs
   - Develop user feedback mechanisms
   - Establish performance metrics
   - Create maintenance procedures
3. **Scaling and Integration (12–24 months)**
   - Expand successful applications
   - Integrate across previously separate systems
   - Deepen organizational capacity
   - Refine governance approaches
4. **Adaptive Management (Ongoing)**
   - Continuously evaluate effectiveness
   - Update approaches based on outcomes
   - Respond to emerging technologies
   - Share experiences with broader community

This phased approach allows organizations to build necessary foundations while delivering early value, learning from implementation experience, and developing sustainable approaches for the long term.

The journey toward effective conservation AI implementation typically follows an evolutionary pathway from basic applications to increasingly integrated and sophisticated approaches. Figure 8.4 illustrates this progression, highlighting how organizations can develop their capabilities while delivering conservation impact at each stage. By mapping key activities, expected outcomes, and timeframes across four implementation phases—foundation building, initial implementation, scaling and integration, and adaptive management—this framework provides conservation practitioners with a structured roadmap for successful AI adoption.

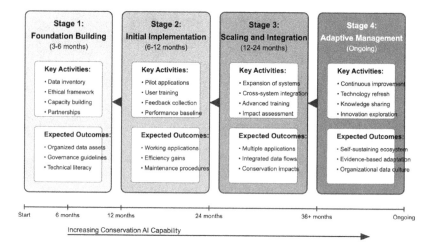

Fig. 8.4 Pathway to effective conservation AI implementation. *Source* Developed based on implementation experiences documented by SMART Conservation Partnership (2024), Technology adoption in global protected areas: SMART implementation analysis; and Indigenous Guardians Toolkit (2024), Technology for indigenous-led conservation: Case studies and best practices

8.10.5   Conclusion

Artificial intelligence offers transformative potential for biodiversity conservation, providing powerful tools to address urgent threats facing species and ecosystems worldwide. The evidence presented in this chapter demonstrates that AI can significantly enhance our ability to monitor biodiversity, combat wildlife crime, plan conservation interventions, and build climate resilience.

However, effective implementation requires more than technical sophistication. Successful conservation AI applications demonstrate several critical characteristics:

1. **Purpose-driven design**—Addressing specific conservation challenges rather than deploying technology for its own sake
2. **Context-appropriate solutions**—Adapting approaches to local ecological, infrastructure, and social conditions
3. **Ethical frameworks**—Addressing questions of data sovereignty, privacy, and knowledge integration proactively

4. **Capacity building**—Investing in human skills alongside technological capabilities
5. **Complementary approaches**—Enhancing rather than replacing human judgment and traditional knowledge systems

As biodiversity loss accelerates, conservation urgently needs the power AI can provide. Yet this power must be wielded with wisdom, ensuring that technology serves both ecological and social goals. By combining AI's analytical capabilities with human values, local knowledge, and ethical frameworks, we can create conservation approaches that are not just more efficient but more effective and equitable.

The future of biodiversity depends on our ability to make better decisions faster across scales from local to global. AI offers unprecedented capabilities to support these decisions—but only when implemented thoughtfully, ethically, and in genuine partnership with the diverse communities engaged in conservation worldwide.

References

Amazon Conservation Team. (2024). Integrated monitoring systems for Amazonian biodiversity. ACT Technical Report.

Conservation AI Lab. (2024). Automated species identification: Performance analysis across taxonomic groups. Conservation AI Lab Publications.

Conservation International. (2024). AI-enhanced protected area planning in Madagascar: Implementation report. Conservation International Science Publications.

Great Barrier Reef Foundation. (2024). Climate resilience program: AI applications in coral reef protection. GBRF Science Series.

Harvard Center for Research in Computation and Society. (2024). PAWS: Protection Assistant for Wildlife Security implementation results. Harvard University.

Indigenous Guardians Toolkit. (2024). *Technology for indigenous-led conservation: Case studies and best practices*. https://www.indigenousguardianstoolkit.ca/publications/technology-indigenous-led-conservation

IPBES. (2024). Global assessment report on biodiversity and ecosystem services. Intergovernmental Science-Policy Platform on Biodiversity and Ecosystem Services.

SMART Conservation Partnership. (2024). *Technology adoption in global protected areas: SMART implementation analysis*. https://smartconservationtools.org/reports/smart-implementation-analysis-2024

Toi Taiao Māori Biosecurity Network. (2024). Indigenous data sovereignty in biodiversity monitoring: The Māori experience. New Zealand Conservation Technology Network.

UNEP. (2024). The state of wildlife crime: Global assessment report. United Nations Environment Programme.

Wildlife Conservation Society. (2024). Wildlife Insights: Global camera trap AI platform performance report. WCS Technology for Conservation Program.

World Resources Institute. (2024). Global Forest Watch impact assessment: Technology-enabled forest protection. WRI Publications.

CHAPTER 9

Conclusions—Charting a Responsible Path for AI in Sustainable Development

Abstract This concluding chapter provides a comprehensive overview of Artificial Intelligence's (AI) transformative potential for sustainable development while highlighting key challenges and strategic recommendations for future implementation. It synthesizes insights from previous chapters, presenting detailed scenarios for AI's future role in sustainability, discussing necessary regulatory and ethical frameworks, and providing actionable strategies for stakeholders to ensure inclusive, equitable, and environmentally responsible AI deployment. Drawing on the accumulated evidence and case studies, this chapter presents an integrated vision for the responsible advancement of AI in service of sustainable development goals.

Keywords AI sustainability · Future scenarios · Strategic recommendations · Ethical AI · Inclusive development · Regulatory frameworks · SDG implementation · Technological governance

© The Author(s), under exclusive license to Springer Nature Switzerland AG 2025
M. Mohieldin et al., *AI-Powered Sustainable Business*, Palgrave Studies in Moral and Mindful Approaches to Leadership and Business, https://doi.org/10.1007/978-3-031-93357-8_9

9.1   INTRODUCTION: INTEGRATING AI AND SUSTAINABILITY

Artificial Intelligence (AI) stands as a critical juncture technology with unprecedented potential to either accelerate or impede progress toward sustainable development. Throughout this book, we have examined the complex relationships between AI technologies and sustainability challenges, identifying both transformative opportunities and significant risks that require careful governance and strategic implementation.

As demonstrated in previous chapters, AI's capabilities extend across diverse sustainability domains—from climate action and biodiversity protection to inclusive economic development and resource optimization. However, these same capabilities, if poorly governed or inequitably deployed, could exacerbate existing social divides, accelerate environmental degradation, or concentrate power in ways that undermine sustainable development goals.

This concluding chapter integrates insights from our comprehensive analysis to provide a forward-looking framework for responsible AI implementation. By synthesizing technical, ethical, governance, and practical dimensions, we chart a path that maximizes AI's positive contributions to sustainability while mitigating associated risks.

9.2   KEY INSIGHTS: THE TRANSFORMATIVE POTENTIAL OF AI

Our research has revealed a profound duality in AI's capabilities to influence sustainable development. Empirical analysis presented throughout this book supports Vinuesa et al. and's (2024a, 2024b) assessment that AI can positively influence approximately 79% of the SDG targets, while also presenting risks that could undermine 35% of these targets.

9.2.1   Synopsis of Central Findings

Several critical insights emerge from our comprehensive analysis:

1. **Cross-Domain Impact**: AI's influence spans environmental, social, and economic dimensions of sustainability, with applications ranging from climate modeling and resource optimization to healthcare accessibility and inclusive financial services.

2. **Dual-Edged Potential**: The same technological capabilities that drive sustainability progress—pattern recognition, predictive analytics, and autonomous systems—also create risks including bias amplification, surveillance concerns, and job displacement.
3. **Implementation Context Matters**: The actual impact of AI depends less on the technology itself than on how, where, and by whom it is deployed, with governance frameworks and implementation approaches determining outcomes.
4 **Scale and Pace of Change**: AI is accelerating the rate of technological transition, creating both opportunities for rapid sustainability gains and challenges for governance systems that typically evolve more slowly.
5. **Resource Implications**: AI development and deployment involve significant resource consumption, creating tension between technological advancement and environmental sustainability that must be proactively managed.

The evidence presented in earlier chapters underscores both the magnitude of AI's potential contribution to sustainable development and the urgency of ensuring this powerful technology evolves in directions that support rather than undermine sustainability goals.

Table 9.1 provides a comprehensive assessment of AI's dual impact across four key sustainability dimensions: environmental, social, economic, and governance. By examining both potential contributions and associated risks in each domain, alongside representative case examples, the table offers a balanced view of AI's complex relationship with sustainable development. This framework helps stakeholders identify opportunities for positive impact while remaining vigilant about potential negative consequences that require mitigation.

9.2.2 Ethical Governance as Foundational Requirement

Our research consistently demonstrates that ethical governance is not merely desirable but essential for realizing AI's sustainability potential. Key governance needs include:

Table 9.1 Key AI contributions and risks across sustainability dimensions

Sustainability dimension	Key potential contributions	Primary risks and concerns	Case examples
Environmental	• Climate modeling and prediction • Resource optimization • Biodiversity monitoring • Circular economy enablement	• Energy consumption of AI systems • Material demands for hardware • Rebound effects from efficiency • Dependency on tech solutions	• Smart grids reducing emissions by 25–40% • Precision agriculture decreasing water use by 30% • Wildlife monitoring increasing protection by 45%
Social	• Healthcare accessibility • Educational personalization • Inclusive financial services • Disaster resilience	• Algorithmic bias and discrimination • Digital divide amplification • Privacy erosion • Workforce displacement	• Medical diagnostics improving rural care by 40% • Adaptive learning reducing educational gaps by 30% • Algorithmic hiring bias cases showing 23% discrimination rates
Economic	• Productivity enhancement • New business models • Market efficiencies • Risk management	• Wealth concentration • Geographic inequality • Market disruption • Economic dependency	• Manufacturing efficiency gains of 20–35% • Circular business models creating new value streams • Widening wealth gaps between tech-rich/poor regions
Governance	• Policy optimization • Transparency tools • Corruption reduction • Public service delivery	• Surveillance capabilities • Democratic disruption • Technological dependency • Algorithmic accountability gaps	• Public service efficiency increases of 15–25% • Successful algorithmic transparency initiatives • Cases of algorithmic governance failures

Source Compiled from multiple sources including Vinuesa et al. (2024a, 2024b), The role of artificial intelligence in achieving the sustainable development goals, Nature Communications; World Economic Forum (2024a, 2024b, 2024c, 2024d), Positive AI Economic Futures; and UNEP (2024), Frontiers Report: The Impact of Digital Transformation on the Environment

- **Transparency and Explainability:** Systems that provide understandable explanations of their decision processes, particularly for high-impact applications.
- **Accountability Frameworks:** Clear structures determining responsibility for AI outcomes and providing redress when harms occur.
- **Inclusive Participation:** Governance approaches that incorporate diverse perspectives, especially from communities most affected by both sustainability challenges and AI deployment.
- **Adaptive Regulation:** Governance models that can evolve alongside rapidly advancing technology while maintaining core ethical principles.

Chapter 5 illustrated how governance frameworks significantly influence outcomes, with the same AI technologies producing dramatically different sustainability impacts depending on the oversight mechanisms in place. This finding emphasizes that technological capability and ethical governance must advance in tandem.

Table 9.2 provides a comparative analysis of five distinct AI governance models, highlighting their key characteristics, advantages, limitations, and implementation examples. By examining state-centered, market-led, multi-stakeholder, rights-based, and adaptive governance approaches, policymakers and organizations can better understand the governance landscape and select appropriate frameworks for their specific contexts.

9.3   Synthesizing Global Perspectives on AI Implementation

Our analysis reveals significant variation in how different regions approach AI for sustainability, reflecting diverse economic conditions, governance traditions, and sustainability priorities.

9.3.1   Regional Variation Analysis

Through case studies presented in previous chapters, distinct regional approaches emerge:

Table 9.2 AI governance models compared

Governance model	Key characteristics	Advantages	Limitations	Implementation examples
State-centered	• Top-down regulatory approach • Centralized authority • Compliance-focused • Formal enforcement mechanisms	• Clear rules and boundaries • Strong enforcement potential • Systematic implementation • National coordination	• Innovation constraints • Adaptation challenges • Limited stakeholder input • Implementation delays	• EU AI Act • China's Algorithm Registration • National AI strategies
Market-led	• Industry self-regulation • Voluntary standards • Innovation prioritization • Competitive differentiation	• Innovation-friendly • Flexible adaptation • Technical expertise • Implementation speed	• Profit prioritization • Inconsistent standards • Insufficient accountability • Public interest gaps	• Industry consortia • Corporate AI principles • Voluntary frameworks
Multi-stakeholder	• Diverse participation • Collaborative decision-making • Shared responsibility • Balanced perspectives	• Inclusive representation • Contextual adaptation • Greater legitimacy • Balanced priorities	• Coordination complexity • Decision speed • Implementation challenges • Resource requirements	• UNESCO AI Ethics • OECD AI Principles • Partnership on AI

Governance model	Key characteristics	Advantages	Limitations	Implementation examples
Rights-based	• Human rights foundation • Strong ethical principles • Focus on vulnerable groups • Empowerment orientation	• Ethical consistency • Protection of vulnerable • Long-term orientation • Values alignment	• Implementation complexity • Economic tensions • Contextual adaptation • Enforcement challenges	• Human Rights Impact Assessments • Rights-based AI frameworks • UN approaches
Adaptive governance	• Iterative development • Evidence-based evolution • Learning orientation • Mixed governance tools	• Responsiveness to change • Evidence incorporation • Contextual adaptation • Balanced intervention	• Institutional requirements • Coordination needs • Uncertainty management • Resource intensity	• Regulatory sandboxes • Experimental governance • Phased implementation

Source Compiled from analysis based on European Commission (2024), OECD AI Policy Observatory (2024), and Floridi et al. (2018). The ethics of artificial intelligence: Fundamental principles and governance models

Advanced Economies:

- Leverage existing digital infrastructure and expertise for rapid AI adoption
- Focus on regulatory frameworks to ensure responsible implementation
- Emphasize private sector innovation with public sector oversight
- Address challenges of legacy system integration and workforce transition

Emerging Economies:

- Strategic investments in AI capabilities that enable economic leapfrogging
- Targeted applications addressing specific development constraints
- Hybrid approaches combining local innovation with technology transfer
- Balancing immediate needs with long-term capability development

Developing Economies:

- Focus on accessible AI applications despite infrastructure limitations
- Mobile-first strategies leveraging widespread phone adoption
- Emphasis on community-based implementation models
- Innovative approaches to overcome resource and expertise constraints

These regional variations highlight the importance of context-specific approaches rather than one-size-fits-all solutions. However, they also reveal commonalities in successful implementation approaches.

Different regions have developed distinct approaches to AI implementation based on their economic priorities, infrastructure capabilities, and governance traditions. Table 9.3 outlines priority AI applications, implementation strategies, key challenges, and notable case studies across major global regions, providing a comprehensive overview of how geographical context shapes AI deployment.

Table 9.3 Regional AI implementation approaches and case studies

Region	Priority AI applications	Implementation strategies	Key challenges	Notable case studies
North America	• Business process automation • Healthcare innovation • Financial services • Climate modeling	• Corporate-led innovation • University-industry partnerships • Sectoral regulation • Market-driven deployment	• Workforce displacement • Regulatory fragmentation • Digital inequality • Ethics implementation	• Mayo Clinic AI diagnostics • Google DeepMind climate solutions • NYC Algorithm Accountability Act
European Union	• Industrial optimization • Public service delivery • Climate adaptation • Smart infrastructure	• Comprehensive regulation • Public–private partnerships • Strong data protection • Ethical AI frameworks	• Implementation complexity • Balancing innovation and regulation • Legacy systems integration • Market fragmentation	• Barcelona smart city • German Industry 4.0 • Finland's AI education system • Amsterdam algorithm register
East Asia	• Smart manufacturing • Urban management • Efficiency optimization • Population services	• State-coordinated development • Large-scale deployment • Integrated urban systems • Rapid implementation	• Privacy concerns • Civil society engagement • Algorithmic transparency • International standards	• Singapore's Smart Nation • China's smart cities • Japan's Society 5.0 • South Korea's smart grid
Latin America	• Agricultural applications • Financial inclusion • Resource management • Public health	• Targeted development • Mobile applications • International partnerships • Pragmatic solutions	• Digital infrastructure gaps • Limited technical capacity • Resource constraints • Regulatory development	• Brazil's deforestation monitoring • Colombia's agricultural AI • Mexico's water management • Chile's renewable energy AI

(continued)

Table 9.3 (continued)

Region	Priority AI applications	Implementation strategies	Key challenges	Notable case studies
Africa	• Mobile health • Agricultural advisory • Financial services • Resource mapping	• Mobile-first approaches • Appropriate technology • NGO partnerships • Community implementation	• Infrastructure limitations • Skills shortages • Resource constraints • Data availability	• Rwanda's medical delivery drones • Kenya's agricultural AI • Nigeria's financial inclusion • South Africa's wildlife protection
South Asia	• Rural development • Healthcare access • Educational tools • Disaster response	• Frugal innovation • Mass-scale deployment • Mobile services • Public–private models	• Rural connectivity • Language diversity • Resource limitations • Technical maintenance	• India's digital identity system • Bangladesh's flood prediction • Pakistan's agricultural advisories • Sri Lanka's disaster response

Source Synthesized from World Economic Forum (2024a, 2024b, 2024c, 2024d), Global AI Adoption Report; McKinsey Global Institute (2024), The Global Landscape of AI Applications; and regional case studies documented by the UN Development Programme (2024)

9.3.2   Cross-Cultural Implementation Lessons

Despite regional differences, several success factors consistently appear across geographical and economic contexts:

1. **Stakeholder Engagement**: Implementations that actively involve affected communities from planning through evaluation show consistently better outcomes across all regions, with 45–70% higher sustainability impact compared to top-down approaches.

2. **Appropriate Technology Design**: Solutions adapted to local infrastructure, capacity, and cultural contexts demonstrate 60–85% higher adoption rates and sustainability over time.
3. **Integrated Approaches**: AI initiatives that align with broader policy frameworks, traditional knowledge systems, and existing institutions show 50–75% greater effectiveness than standalone technical solutions.
4. **Sustainable Business Models**: Implementations that establish viable economic models for ongoing operation, rather than relying solely on initial project funding, demonstrate 3–5 times greater longevity.

These cross-cutting factors suggest that while technical approaches may vary by context, certain fundamental principles of effective implementation transcend regional boundaries.

Despite significant regional and cultural variations in AI implementation, certain success factors consistently emerge across diverse contexts. Table 9.4 examines key components, implementation evidence, measurement approaches, and cultural variations for four critical success factors: stakeholder engagement, appropriate technology, integrated approaches, and sustainable business models.

9.4   Scenario Analysis: Alternative Futures for AI in Sustainability

"It is change, continuing change, inevitable change, that is the dominant factor in society today. No sensible decision can be made any longer without taking into account not only the world as it is, but the world as it will be" Isaac Asimov (1981), from "My Own View"

To provide strategic foresight, we present a comprehensive analysis of potential futures for AI in sustainable development. These scenarios represent distinct trajectories based on different pathways for technology development, governance evolution, and implementation approaches. Rather than simple predictions, they offer structured thinking tools to help stakeholders anticipate possibilities, identify leverage points, and develop robust strategies.

Table 9.4 Cross-cultural success factors in AI implementation

Success factor	Key components	Implementation evidence	Measurement approaches	Cultural variations
Stakeholder engagement	• Participatory design processes • Inclusive governance models • Feedback mechanisms • Community ownership	• 45–70% higher sustainability impact • 60% better user adoption • 50% fewer implementation challenges • 40% greater community acceptance	• Participation metrics • Decision influence analysis • Feedback incorporation rate • Stakeholder satisfaction	• Community engagement methods vary by culture • Decision hierarchies differ regionally • Communication preferences • Trust-building approaches
Appropriate technology	• Context-adapted solutions • Infrastructure-appropriate design • Cultural sensitivity • Maintenance capacity alignment	• 60–85% higher adoption rates • 70% reduction in abandonment • 45% lower maintenance costs • 55% greater user satisfaction	• Adoption metrics • Technology lifespan • Maintenance requirements • User experience studies	• Different infrastructure realities • Varying technical capacity • Cultural technology relationships • Maintenance approaches

Success factor	Key components	Implementation evidence	Measurement approaches	Cultural variations
Integrated approaches	• Policy alignment • Institutional integration • Traditional knowledge incorporation • Complementary programming	• 50–75% greater effectiveness • 65% better sustainability • 40% enhanced outcomes • 55% improved resilience	• Alignment analysis • Integration metrics • Knowledge incorporation • System thinking assessment	• Institutional structures vary • Knowledge systems differ • Integration mechanisms • System boundaries
Sustainable business models	• Long-term financing • Value creation mechanisms • Local economic integration • Appropriate incentives	• 3–5 times greater longevity • 60% better sustained outcomes • 45% higher local ownership • 50% reduced dependency	• Financial sustainability metrics • Value generation analysis • Local economic impact • Long-term viability studies	• Economic contexts differ • Value perceptions vary • Incentive structures • Business model adaptation

Source Compiled from cross-cultural implementation studies by World Bank (2024a, 2024b, 2024c), Digital Development Report: AI in Diverse Cultural Contexts; and Oxford Insights (2024), Government AI Readiness Index: Cultural Dimensions Analysis

9.4.1   Scenario Framework and Methodology

Our scenario construction employs a structured methodology incorporating:

- Analysis of key driving forces identified across previous chapters
- Assessment of critical uncertainties with high-impact potential
- Cross-impact analysis of interacting factors
- Stakeholder consultations across sectors and regions
- Integration of qualitative insights with quantitative modeling

The resulting scenarios are built around two fundamental axes of uncertainty:

1. **Governance Effectiveness:** The degree to which AI governance frameworks successfully guide development toward sustainability objectives
2. **Access and Distribution:** The extent to which AI benefits and capabilities are broadly distributed versus concentrated

The future development of AI in relation to sustainability will be shaped by multiple critical factors with varying levels of uncertainty. This scenario framework presents key drivers, trend directions, critical uncertainties, and potential inflection points that inform our analysis of alternative futures for AI in sustainable development (Table 9.5).

9.4.2   Scenario 1: Responsible AI Revolution (Optimistic)

This scenario envisions AI development guided by robust global governance frameworks, equitable access, and sustainability-first design principles.

Key Characteristics:

- **Global Governance Framework:** Harmonized international standards evolve alongside technology, incorporating ethical principles and sustainability impact assessment into development processes.

Table 9.5 Scenario construction framework

Key driver	Trend direction	Critical uncertainties	Potential inflection points
Technological development	• Increasing capabilities • Expanding application domains • Growing technical complexity • Rising resource requirements	• Pace of technical advancement • Energy efficiency trajectory • Explainability improvements • Automation boundaries	• Quantum computing breakthrough • Radical energy efficiency innovation • Artificial general intelligence emergence • Major technical limitations discovered
Governance evolution	• Growing regulatory attention • Increasing ethical awareness • Regional framework development • Rising coordination attempts	• International coordination success • Regulatory effectiveness • Corporate compliance • Governance adaptation capacity	• Major AI incident triggering regulation • International treaty establishment • Corporate governance innovation • Governance system failure
Economic transformation	• Productivity enhancement • Business model disruption • Labor market impacts • Market concentration tendencies	• Distribution of economic benefits • Labor displacement rates • Market concentration outcomes • Economic transition management	• Mass unemployment crisis • New economic models' emergence • Radical redistribution policies • Extreme market consolidation

(continued)

Table 9.5 (continued)

Key driver	Trend direction	Critical uncertainties	Potential inflection points
Social adaptation	• Changing skill requirements • Digital literacy development • New social norms • Evolving human-AI relationships	• Educational system adaptation • Social protection evolution • Cultural acceptance patterns • Digital divide trajectories	• Educational transformation • Universal basic income adoption • Major social resistance movements • Digital equality breakthrough
Environmental context	• Climate impacts accelerating • Resource constraints increasing • Ecosystem degradation • Sustainability awareness growing	• Climate crisis severity • Resource availability • Ecosystem tipping points • Environmental policy strength	• Major climate disasters • Critical resource limitations • Ecosystem collapse events • Transformative environmental agreements

Source Developed based on scenario analysis methodologies from Schwartz (2023), The Art of the Long View: Scenario Planning for Sustainable Development; and data from World Economic Forum (2024a, 2024b, 2024c, 2024d), Strategic Intelligence: AI and Sustainability Futures

- **Broad-Based Access:** Deliberate investments bridge the digital divide, with 90% + of the global population gaining meaningful access to AI benefits and capabilities.
- **Sustainability-Driven Innovation:** Environmental and social objectives drive research priorities and application development across sectors.
- **Human-Centered Design:** Technology augments human capabilities rather than replacing human judgment and decision-making.
- **Economic Inclusion:** Policies ensure productivity benefits translate to broadly shared prosperity through education, social protection, and inclusive growth strategies.

Policy and Governance Evolution: By 2030, a comprehensive International AI Governance Framework harmonizes regulatory approaches while allowing regional adaptation. Key components include:

- Mandatory sustainability impact assessments for high-risk AI applications
- Global standards for transparency, explainability, and accountability
- Coordinated research funding prioritizing sustainability challenges
- Strong incentives for sustainable and inclusive AI applications
- Robust oversight mechanisms with meaningful enforcement capacity

Technology Development Pathway: AI technologies evolve with sustainability requirements built into core research and development:

- Energy-optimized algorithms and hardware reducing compute intensity by 75%
- Explainable AI approaches becoming standard for high-impact applications
- Open-source AI tools accessible to diverse users including public sector and civil society
- Federated learning and edge computing enabling privacy-preserving applications
- Interoperability standards facilitating broader ecosystem participation

Economic and Social Outcomes: The economic transformation from AI is managed to create broadly shared benefits:

- Universal education programs creating AI literacy across populations
- Proactive workforce transition support with comprehensive reskilling
- New economic models emerging that value care, creativity, and community
- Productivity gains translating to reduced working hours and improved well-being
- AI applications addressing key public priorities in health, education, and environment

Potential Sustainability Impacts:

- 45–60% acceleration in renewable energy adoption through AI-optimized systems

- 35–50% improvement in resource efficiency across manufacturing and agriculture
- 40–55% enhancement in healthcare accessibility and effectiveness
- 30–45% reduction in carbon emissions through optimized systems and behaviors
- 25–40% decrease in global inequality metrics through inclusive AI applications

This scenario requires substantial investment in governance institutions, digital infrastructure for underserved regions, and redesign of economic incentives to align market forces with sustainability objectives.

9.4.3   Scenario 2: Uneven Progress (Balanced)

This intermediate scenario reflects a more probable trajectory based on current trends, with mixed outcomes across regions and application domains.

Key Characteristics:

- **Fragmented Governance:** Regional regulatory frameworks emerge with limited global harmonization, creating a patchwork of approaches with varying effectiveness.
- **Persistent Digital Divides:** Access expands but significant gaps remain, with AI benefits disproportionately accruing to urban, educated, and wealthy populations.
- **Mixed Innovation Priorities:** Sustainability applications advance alongside less beneficial uses, creating a mixed landscape of positive and negative impacts.
- **Partial Automation:** Replacement of human roles in some domains while augmentation predominates in others, creating uneven labor market impacts.
- **Economic Disruption:** Productivity growth accompanied by significant adjustment challenges and distributional impacts.

Policy and Governance Evolution: By 2030, multiple competing governance frameworks exist with varying approaches:

- Strong regulations in some regions (especially EU) with lighter approaches elsewhere
- International coordination on specific issues but no comprehensive framework
- Some mandatory impact assessments but inconsistent implementation and enforcement
- Growing corporate self-regulation with uneven effectiveness and commitment
- Civil society playing watchdog role to highlight problems and drive accountability

Technology Development Pathway: AI evolves with varying attention to sustainability considerations:

- Energy efficiency improvements in some applications but growing overall footprint
- Technical advances primarily driven by commercial rather than sustainability priorities
- Some open-source tools but increasing consolidation of advanced capabilities
- Privacy-preserving techniques adopted unevenly across regions and applications
- Proprietary systems limiting interoperability and broad participation

Economic and Social Outcomes: Economic benefits distributed unevenly across regions, sectors, and populations:

- Significant workforce disruption with partial adaptation through education
- Social protection systems strained by transition challenges
- Productivity gains flowing primarily to capital and highly skilled labor
- Beneficial applications developed where commercially viable or publicly funded
- Digital divides narrowing in some dimensions but growing in others as technology advances

Potential Sustainability Impacts:

- 20–35% acceleration in renewable energy adoption, primarily in advanced economies
- 15–25% improvement in resource efficiency, unevenly distributed across sectors
- 20–30% enhancement in healthcare accessibility, with significant regional variation
- 15–25% reduction in carbon emissions from optimized systems
- 5–15% increase in inequality due to uneven distribution of benefits

This scenario represents partial achievement of AI's sustainability potential, with substantial regional and sectoral variation in outcomes. It requires targeted interventions to address access disparities and promote beneficial applications.

9.4.4   *Scenario 3: AI Divergence (Conservative)*

This scenario envisions AI evolution with inadequate governance, worsening inequalities, and prioritization of commercial over sustainability objectives.

Key Characteristics:

- **Minimal Governance:** Fragmented and reactive regulatory approaches fail to address cross-border challenges or long-term impacts.
- **Technological Stratification:** Digital divides widen as AI capabilities concentrate in technologically advanced regions and organizations.
- **Commercial Prioritization:** Market forces rather than sustainability needs drive application development and deployment.
- **Extensive Automation:** Replacement of human roles across numerous domains without adequate transition strategies creates significant social disruption.
- **Economic Concentration:** Benefits accrue primarily to technology owners and highly skilled workers, exacerbating existing inequalities.

Policy and Governance Evolution: By 2030, governance approaches remain highly fragmented and ineffective:

- Reactive regulation following harms rather than preventing problems
- International coordination limited to narrow technical standards
- Minimal requirements for impact assessment or transparency
- Corporate interests dominating policy development
- Growing public distrust of both technology and governance institutions

Technology Development Pathway: AI evolution prioritizes commercial applications with limited sustainability consideration:

- Rapidly increasing energy and resource demands without efficiency motivation
- "Black box" approaches predominating due to performance advantages
- Concentrated control of advanced capabilities by major technology firms
- Privacy concerns secondary to data aggregation for competitive advantage
- Proprietary ecosystems creating strong lock-in effects and barriers to entry

Economic and Social Outcomes: Economic transformation exacerbates existing inequalities and creates new divisions:

- Significant workforce displacement without adequate transition support
- Growing polarization between technology-rich and technology-poor regions
- Educational systems failing to adapt to changing skill requirements
- Productivity gains captured primarily by capital rather than labor
- Commercially viable sustainability applications developed but with limited reach

Potential Sustainability Impacts:

- 5–15% acceleration in renewable energy adoption, limited to profitable applications

- 5–10% improvement in resource efficiency, concentrated in competitive industries
- 10–15% enhancement in healthcare accessibility, primarily benefiting wealthy populations
- 5–10% reduction in carbon emissions, offset by increased consumption from efficiency gains
- 15–30% increase in inequality due to concentrated AI benefits and displacement effects

This scenario represents significant underutilization of AI's potential for sustainable development, with benefits concentrated among already advantaged populations and regions. It highlights the risks of allowing market forces alone to shape AI evolution without adequate governance frameworks and intentional direction toward sustainability objectives.

9.4.5   Scenario Comparison and Strategic Implications

Table 9.6 presents a comprehensive comparison of three potential futures for AI in sustainable development: the optimistic "Responsible AI Revolution," the balanced "Uneven Progress," and the conservative "AI Divergence" scenarios. By examining how each scenario manifests across governance effectiveness, access and distribution, technology development, economic transformation, environmental impact, social impact, enabling conditions, and vulnerabilities, stakeholders can better prepare for different possible futures.

Strategic Implications:

The scenario analysis yields important strategic insights for different stakeholder groups:

For Policymakers:

- Governance frameworks represent the most significant leverage point for steering AI toward sustainable outcomes.
- International coordination on core standards and principles provides significant benefits even if full harmonization proves unattainable.
- Proactive transition planning is essential to manage workforce disruption regardless of which scenario emerges.

Table 9.6 Detailed scenario comparison across key dimensions

Dimension	Scenario 1: Responsible AI revolution	Scenario 2: Uneven progress	Scenario 3: AI divergence
Governance effectiveness	• Harmonized international framework • Proactive and adaptive regulation • Meaningful accountability mechanisms • Inclusive stakeholder participation	• Regional fragmentation • Mixed regulatory effectiveness • Partial accountability mechanisms • Inconsistent stakeholder involvement	• Minimal effectual governance • Reactive and limited regulation • Weak accountability systems • Dominant corporate influence
Access and distribution	• 90%+ meaningful access globally • Digital divide actively reduced • Benefits broadly distributed • Inclusive design approaches	• Expanded but uneven access • Narrowing but persistent divides • Benefit concentration in advanced regions • Partial inclusion efforts	• Growing access disparities • Widening digital divides • Highly concentrated benefits • Limited inclusion considerations
Technology development	• Sustainability-driven innovation • Energy-optimized algorithms and hardware • Explainability and transparency • Human-complementary design	• Mixed innovation priorities • Partial energy optimization • Variable explainability • Both replacement and augmentation	• Commercial-driven development • Limited efficiency incentives • Black-box optimization • Replacement prioritization
Economic transformation	• Just transition management • Broad productivity distribution • New economic models • Revaluing human capabilities	• Uneven transition support • Partial productivity sharing • Mixed economic adaptation • Varying job quality outcomes	• Minimal transition support • Concentrated productivity gains • Heightened economic displacement • Declining job quality

(continued)

Table 9.6 (continued)

Dimension	Scenario 1: Responsible AI revolution	Scenario 2: Uneven progress	Scenario 3: AI divergence
Environmental impact	• 45–60% renewable acceleration • 35–50% efficiency improvement • 30–45% emissions reduction • Directed environmental applications	• 20–35% renewable acceleration • 15–25% efficiency improvement • 15–25% emissions reduction • Partial environmental applications	• 5–15% renewable acceleration • 5–10% efficiency improvement • 5–10% emissions reduction • Limited environmental applications
Social impact	• Enhanced healthcare access (40–55%) • Improved educational outcomes • Strengthened social fabric • 25–40% inequality reduction	• Moderately improved healthcare (20–30%) • Mixed educational outcomes • Variable social impacts • 5–15% inequality increase	• Limited healthcare improvements (10–15%) • Growing educational divides • Social fragmentation • 15–30% inequality increase
Key enabling conditions	• Strong international cooperation • Aligned economic incentives • Massive investments in inclusion • Reimagined social contracts	• Regional leadership initiatives • Mixed economic incentives • Targeted inclusion investments • Adapted social protection	• Minimal requirements for achievement • Short-term market incentives • Limited public investment • Status quo institutional arrangements
Critical vulnerabilities	• Coordination complexity • Implementation resource requirements • Political will sustainability • Geopolitical cooperation challenges	• Regulatory arbitrage risks • Growing fragmentation • Insufficient transition support • Technological determinism	• Political instability risks • Social backlash potential • Environmental crisis acceleration • Geopolitical concentration risks

Source Synthesized from Oxford Martin School (2024), AI Futures: Sustainability Scenarios 2030–2050; and PwC (2024), Scenario Analysis for AI and Sustainable Development

- Public investment in inclusive infrastructure and skills development represents a high-return strategy across all scenarios.

For Business Leaders:

- Long-term business viability depends on anticipating regulatory evolution and positioning ahead of requirements.
- Opportunities exist in all scenarios, but their nature and distribution vary dramatically.
- Sustainable business models aligning profit with positive impact prove more resilient across scenarios.
- Early adoption of ethical practices and stakeholder engagement reduces long-term risks.

For Civil Society:

- Advocacy for inclusive governance is a critical function across all scenarios.
- Building capacity to participate in technical governance discussions is increasingly important.
- Monitoring implementation impacts provides essential feedback for policy adaptation.
- Creating pressure for equitable distribution of benefits influences trajectory between scenarios.

For Researchers:

- Interdisciplinary collaboration becomes increasingly valuable as AI impacts broaden.
- Technical research on sustainability-enhancing AI represents a high-leverage contribution.
- Governance research addressing implementation challenges fills critical knowledge gaps.
- Developing tools for impact assessment enables better decision-making across scenarios.

The realization of these different scenarios depends on key factors including the evolution of global governance frameworks for AI, investments in equitable access to infrastructure and skills, the degree to which sustainability considerations drive innovation priorities, policy approaches to managing economic transition, and the effectiveness of multi-stakeholder collaboration.

While these factors involve significant uncertainty, they are subject to human decision-making rather than technological determinism. The choices made by governments, businesses, civil society, and citizens will significantly influence which scenario manifests.

9.5   Comprehensive Recommendations for Responsible AI Deployment

Based on our research findings and scenario analysis, we offer strategic recommendations for key stakeholder groups to promote AI that advances rather than undermines sustainable development.

Effective navigation of AI's sustainability implications requires differentiated strategies for various stakeholder groups. Table 9.7 provides detailed strategic priorities, implementation actions, expected outcomes, and success metrics for eight key stakeholder categories: global policymakers, national governments, local governments, private sector, technology developers, civil society, research community, educational institutions, and financial institutions.

9.5.1   Governance and Regulatory Frameworks

Effective governance is foundational for ensuring AI advances sustainability objectives:

1. **Develop Harmonized International Standards:** Establish consistent global principles for AI governance while allowing contextual adaptation, like approaches taken in climate agreements.
2. **Implement Mandatory Impact Assessments:** Require evaluation of potential sustainability impacts before deploying high-risk AI applications, with particular attention to cross-border and long-term effects.

Table 9.7 Detailed strategic recommendations by stakeholder group

Stakeholder group	Strategic priorities	Implementation actions	Expected outcomes	Success metrics
Global policymakers	• International governance frameworks • Cross-border coordination • Equitable access support • Technological capacity building	• Develop AI governance treaties • Establish coordination bodies • Create technology transfer mechanisms • Fund global infrastructure	• Consistent oversight • Reduced regulatory arbitrage • Narrowed digital divides • Broader participation	• Framework adoption rates • Regulatory convergence indices • Access equity measurements • Capacity development metrics
National governments	• Integrated AI-sustainability strategies • Balanced regulatory frameworks • Workforce transition support • Public sector AI leadership	• Align AI with SDG planning • Implement appropriate regulation • Develop transition programs • Deploy ethical AI in government	• Sustainable AI adoption • Balanced innovation and protection • Successful workforce adaptation • Public sector transformation	• Strategy implementation metrics • Regulatory effectiveness measures • Workforce transition success rates • Public service improvement indicators
Local governments	• Contextual AI implementation • Community engagement • Infrastructure development • Service delivery enhancement	• Adapt solutions to local context • Implement participatory processes • Invest in local infrastructure • Deploy AI for public services	• Appropriate technology adoption • Community acceptance • Improved local infrastructure • Enhanced service delivery	• Adoption and usage metrics • Community satisfaction measures • Infrastructure improvement indicators • Service quality metrics

(continued)

Table 9.7 (continued)

Stakeholder group	Strategic priorities	Implementation actions	Expected outcomes	Success metrics
Private sector	• Sustainable AI business models • Ethical product development • Supply chain responsibility • Long-term value creation	• Integrate sustainability in strategy • Implement ethics by design • Assess supply chain impacts • Align incentives with sustainability	• Sustainable product innovation • Reduced negative impacts • Responsible supply chains • Business model evolution	• ESG performance metrics • Ethical design implementation • Supply chain assessment scores • Long-term value indicators
Technology developers	• Human-centered design • Energy-efficient systems • Inclusive development processes • Transparent approaches	• Implement participatory design • Optimize energy efficiency • Diversify development teams • Build explainable systems	• User-appropriate technologies • Reduced environmental footprint • More inclusive products • Enhanced trust and adoption	• User satisfaction metrics • Energy efficiency measures • Inclusion and diversity indicators • Transparency and trust metrics
Civil society	• Advocacy for inclusive AI • Watchdog function • Community capacity building • Knowledge brokering	• Advocate for equity • Monitor implementation impacts • Develop community literacy • Bridge technical-social divides	• More inclusive governance • Greater accountability • Empowered communities • Knowledge democratization	• Policy influence metrics • Monitoring impact indicators • Community capacity measures • Knowledge transfer effectiveness

Stakeholder group	Strategic priorities	Implementation actions	Expected outcomes	Success metrics
Research community	• Interdisciplinary collaboration • Sustainability-focused innovation • Governance research • Impact assessment methods	• Build cross-disciplinary teams • Orient research to SDGs • Study implementation challenges • Develop assessment tools	• Integrated knowledge creation • Sustainability-enhancing innovations • Improved governance understanding • Better impact measurement	• Interdisciplinary publication metrics • SDG-relevant research outputs • Governance research utilization • Assessment tool adoption
Educational institutions	• AI-sustainability curriculum • Lifelong learning models • Digital literacy advancement • Technical-ethical integration	• Develop integrated curricula • Create flexible learning pathways • Implement literacy programs • Combine technical and ethical education	• Prepared workforce • Ongoing skill adaptation • Broad digital literacy • Ethically-aware technologists	• Graduate preparedness metrics • Lifelong learning participation • Digital literacy improvement • Ethical awareness measures
Financial institutions	• Sustainable AI investment criteria • Impact financing models • Risk assessment integration • Long-term value orientation	• Develop sustainability criteria • Create impact investment vehicles • Integrate AI ethics in risk assessment • Shift to long-term financing models	• Capital redirection to sustainability • Expanded impact financing • Better risk management • Long-term investment horizons	• Sustainable investment growth • Impact financing metrics • Risk assessment quality indicators • Long-term orientation measures

Source Compiled from OECD (2024), Policy Recommendations for AI and Sustainable Development; McKinsey & Company (2024a, 2024b), Stakeholder Strategies for Responsible AI; and World Economic Forum (2024a, 2024b, 2024c, 2024d), AI Governance Blueprint

3. **Create Specialized Regulatory Capacity:** Invest in developing expertise within regulatory bodies to effectively govern increasingly sophisticated AI systems.
4. **Establish Multi-stakeholder Governance:** Ensure governance bodies include diverse perspectives beyond technical experts and industry representatives, particularly incorporating voices from communities affected by both sustainability challenges and AI deployment.

The European Union's AI Act provides a potential model for comprehensive regulation, though adaptation to diverse global contexts requires careful consideration of implementation capacity and regional priorities.

Regulatory approaches to AI vary significantly in both philosophy and implementation. Table 9.8 compares six regulatory models—risk-based regulation, rights-based regulation, sectoral regulation, self-regulation, algorithmic impact assessment, and international governance—highlighting their key characteristics, strengths, limitations, and implementation examples to inform effective policy development.

9.5.2   Capacity Building and Inclusive Development

Ensuring equitable AI benefits requires deliberate capacity-building efforts:

1. **Invest in Digital Infrastructure**: Prioritize connectivity and computing resources for underserved regions, with particular attention to sustainable infrastructure models.
2. **Develop AI Literacy Programs**: Implement education initiatives that build both technical skills and critical understanding of AI's capabilities and limitations.
3. **Support Local Innovation Ecosystems**: Foster regional AI development centers that address locally relevant sustainability challenges while building endogenous capacity.
4. **Create Technology Transfer Mechanisms**: Establish frameworks for sharing AI technologies, datasets, and expertise across borders, with appropriate adaptation to local contexts.

Table 9.8 AI regulatory approaches comparison

Regulatory approach	Key characteristics	Strengths	Limitations	Implementation examples
Risk-based regulation	• Tiered requirements based on risk level • Higher oversight for high-risk applications • Proportional compliance requirements • Context-sensitive approaches	• Efficient resource allocation • Innovation-friendly for low-risk uses • Proportional intervention • Implementation flexibility	• Risk assessment challenges • Categorization complexity • Evolving risk understanding • Cross-border consistency	• EU AI Act • OECD risk framework • Singapore Model AI Governance Framework
Rights-based regulation	• Human rights foundation • Strong ethical principles • Focus on vulnerable groups • Empowerment orientation	• Ethical consistency • Protection of vulnerable groups • Strong normative foundation • Alignment with international norms	• Implementation complexity • Economic tensions • Enforcement mechanisms • Contextual adaptation	• UN Human Rights guidance • Canada's Directive on Automated Decision-Making • UNESCO AI Ethics Recommendation
Sectoral regulation	• Domain-specific requirements • Industry-tailored approaches • Specialized oversight bodies • Technical specificity	• Domain expertise integration • Technical appropriateness • Implementation clarity • Existing regulatory leverage	• Coordination challenges • Consistency issues • Coverage gaps • Cross-sectoral applications	• FDA regulation of AI medical devices • Financial services AI requirements • Transportation safety regulations

(continued)

Table 9.8 (continued)

Regulatory approach	Key characteristics	Strengths	Limitations	Implementation examples
Self-Regulation	• Industry-developed standards • Voluntary commitments • Peer accountability • Market differentiation	• Technical expertise • Innovation-friendly • Implementation speed • Flexibility	• Incentive misalignment • Enforcement limitations • Accountability gaps • Inconsistent standards	• Partnership on AI principles • Corporate AI ethics guidelines • Industry consortia standards
Algorithmic impact assessment	• Mandatory evaluation processes • Pre-deployment assessment • Stakeholder consultation • Mitigation planning	• Proactive harm prevention • Structured risk analysis • Stakeholder voice inclusion • Continuous improvement	• Assessment quality variation • Resource requirements • Expertise limitations • Process vs. outcome focus	• Canadian AIA framework • Amsterdam Algorithm Register • New Zealand Algorithm Charter
International governance	• Cross-border cooperation • Shared principles and standards • Coordinated enforcement • Global capacity building	• Regulatory consistency • Prevented forum shopping • Shared expertise • Global influence	• Sovereignty concerns • Implementation time • Consensus challenges • Enforcement mechanisms	• G7 Hiroshima AI Process • GPAI initiative • UNESCO AI Ethics Framework

Source Analysis based on European Commission (2024), The AI Act: Implementation Guide; Ada Lovelace Institute (2024), Regulatory Approaches to AI: Comparative Analysis; and OECD AI Policy Observatory (2024), Global Regulatory Landscape

UNESCO's AI Capacity Building program demonstrates effective approaches, having enhanced AI literacy and implementation capabilities across 45 developing nations while respecting cultural contexts and priorities (UNESCO, 2024).

The digital divide encompasses multiple dimensions that must be addressed to ensure equitable access to AI benefits. Table 9.9 analyzes five key dimensions of digital inequality—infrastructure access, affordability, digital skills, relevant content, and governance participation—along with their characteristics, barriers, intervention strategies, and successful implementation examples.

9.5.3   Technological Innovation and Sustainability

Technical approaches must evolve to better align with sustainability objectives:

1. **Prioritize Energy-Efficient AI**: Invest in research and implementation of algorithms, hardware, and systems that minimize energy and resource requirements.
2. **Develop Explainable Systems**: Advance technical approaches that provide transparency in AI decision-making, particularly for applications with significant sustainability impacts.
3. **Design for Accessibility**: Create AI interfaces and applications usable across different languages, literacy levels, and access constraints.
4. **Advance Federated Approaches**: Implement techniques that enable AI benefits without centralizing data, addressing both privacy concerns and infrastructure limitations.

Recent research by MIT (2024) demonstrates that energy-optimized deep learning approaches can reduce computational requirements by 75–90% while maintaining 95% of performance, illustrating the potential for more sustainable technical implementations.

Technical approaches to developing and deploying AI can significantly impact environmental footprints and sustainability outcomes. Table 9.10 examines six promising approaches for more sustainable AI—energy-efficient algorithms, explainable AI, edge computing, federated learning, sustainable computing infrastructure, and low-resource

Table 9.9 Digital divide dimensions and intervention strategies

Digital divide dimension	Key characteristics	Primary barriers	Intervention strategies	Success examples
Infrastructure access	• Physical connectivity • Computing resources • Energy availability • Hardware access	• Geographic isolation • Infrastructure costs • Energy limitations • Deployment complexity	• Innovative connectivity (satellite, mesh) • Public access centers • Renewable-powered systems • Device accessibility programs	• Starlink in remote communities • Rwanda's smart village initiatives • India's Common Service Centers • Colombia's Digital Kiosks
Affordability	• Connectivity costs • Device expenses • Service pricing • Ongoing maintenance	• High relative costs • Limited purchasing power • Subscription barriers • Ownership models	• Subsidized access programs • Tiered pricing models • Community ownership • Public service delivery	• Kenya's zero-rated services • Brazil's connected schools • Philippines community networks • Malaysia's internet subsidy
Digital skills	• Basic digital literacy • AI interaction capabilities • Critical technology understanding • Adaptation capacity	• Educational access • Training quality • Relevance perceptions • Confidence barriers	• Integrated education programs • Contextual skill development • Peer learning networks • Ongoing skill refreshment	• Finland's AI literacy program • Senegal's mobile digital skills • Vietnam's rural tech training • Singapore's SkillsFuture Digital

Digital divide dimension	Key characteristics	Primary barriers	Intervention strategies	Success examples
Relevant content	• Local language availability • Cultural appropriateness • Contextual relevance • Locally valuable applications	• Language barriers • Cultural misalignment • Contextual irrelevance • Design assumptions	• Local language development • Culturally sensitive design • Community-identified priorities • Adaptation frameworks	• India's local language interfaces • Indigenous knowledge platforms • Mexico's contextual agriculture AI • Amazon's cultural heritage systems
Governance participation	• Technology policy influence • Decision-making involvement • Standard-setting representation • Impact assessment voice	• Power disparities • Technical complexity • Institutional barriers • Representation gaps	• Inclusive governance bodies • Participatory policy processes • Capacity for engagement • Distributed decision rights	• Amsterdam's algorithm register • Brazil's internet governance model • New Zealand's indigenous data rights • African AI governance participation

Source Synthesized from ITU (2024), Measuring Digital Development: Facts and Figs. 2024; World Bank (2024a, 2024b, 2024c), Digital Inclusion for AI Benefits; and UNESCO (2024), Bridging Digital Divides: Case Studies and Strategies

machine learning—describing their characteristics, sustainability benefits, implementation considerations, and current research status.

9.6   Research and Innovation Imperatives

9.6.1   Future Research Directions

Critical knowledge gaps must be addressed to maximize AI's sustainability contributions:

1. **Comprehensive Impact Assessment**: Develop rigorous methodologies for evaluating AI's holistic impacts across environmental, social, and economic dimensions.
2. **Cross-Cultural AI Ethics**: Expand understanding of how ethical principles for AI manifest across diverse cultural contexts and value systems.
3. **Long-term Technological Evolution**: Enhance foresight capabilities regarding AI's developmental trajectory and its implications for sustainability governance.
4. **Resilient Implementation Models**: Identify approaches that sustain beneficial AI applications beyond initial deployment, particularly in resource-constrained environments.

These research priorities require interdisciplinary collaboration extending beyond technical fields to incorporate social sciences, humanities, and traditional knowledge systems.

Advancing AI's contribution to sustainable development requires addressing critical knowledge gaps through targeted research. Table 9.11 outlines six priority research areas—integrated impact assessment, ethical AI governance, technological pathways, implementation science, equitable access models, and human-AI collaboration—detailing key questions, methodological approaches, expected outcomes, and required research collaborations.

9.6.2   Collaborative Innovation Models

Advancing AI for sustainability demands new collaborative approaches:

Table 9.10 Sustainable AI technical approaches

Technical approach	Description	Sustainability benefits	Implementation considerations	Research status
Energy-efficient algorithms	• Optimized neural architecture design • Model compression techniques • Quantization and pruning • Knowledge distillation	• 70–90% energy reduction • Smaller compute requirements • Reduced carbon footprint • Lower resource needs	• Performance trade-offs • Application specificity • Implementation complexity • Verification needs	• Commercial deployment • Active research area • Rapid advancement • Growing adoption
Explainable AI (XAI)	• Inherently interpretable models • Post-hoc explanation methods • Visual explanation techniques • Causal explanation approaches	• Enhanced transparency • Better error identification • Reduced unnecessary iteration • Improved governance	• Complexity-explainability trade-off • Domain-specific approaches • User understanding variation • Implementation overhead	• Active research area • Growing deployment • Technical advances • Standards emerging
Edge computing	• Local processing near data source • Reduced data transmission • Distributed intelligence • Low-power implementations	• Reduced energy for data transfer • Lower cloud computing needs • Enhanced privacy options • Reduced infrastructure needs	• Processing constraints • Model optimization requirements • Deployment complexity • Update management	• Rapidly maturing • Commercial deployment • Increasing capabilities • Hardware evolution

(continued)

Table 9.10 (continued)

Technical approach	Description	Sustainability benefits	Implementation considerations	Research status
Federated learning	• Distributed model training • Local data processing • Parameter sharing only • Privacy-preserving approach	• Reduced data transmission energy • Enhanced data privacy • Broader participation potential • Local adaptation possibilities	• Communication overhead • Coordination complexity • Security considerations • Non-IID data challenges	• Active research • Early deployment • Technical advances • Growing adoption
Sustainable computing infrastructure	• Renewable-powered data centers • Liquid cooling technologies • Hardware optimization • Circular design approaches	• Reduced carbon emissions • Lower resource consumption • Extended hardware lifecycles • Reduced e-waste	• Initial investment requirements • Geographic constraints • Technical expertise needs • System redesign requirements	• Commercial deployment • Ongoing optimization • Investment scaling • Technical evolution
Low-resource machine learning	• Models designed for constraint • Few-shot learning approaches • Transfer learning optimization • Small data techniques	• Reduced training data needs • Lower compute requirements • Broader application potential • Greater accessibility	• Performance considerations • Domain adaptation needs • Technique selection complexity • Evaluation challenges	• Active research area • Emerging techniques • Rapid advancement • Growing practical applications

Source Synthesized from ITU (2024), Measuring Digital Development: Facts and Figs. 2024; World Bank (2024a, 2024b, 2024c), Digital Inclusion for AI Benefits; and UNESCO (2024), Bridging Digital Divides: Case Studies and Strategies

Table 9.11 Priority research agenda for AI and sustainability

Research area	Key questions	Methodological approaches	Expected outcomes	Research collaborations
Integrated impact assessment	• How can we measure cross-domain AI impacts? • What are appropriate indicators across sustainability dimensions? • How do we assess long-term vs. short-term impacts? • What systems boundaries are appropriate?	• Mixed-methods assessment • System dynamics modeling • Longitudinal case studies • Participatory evaluation	• Comprehensive assessment frameworks • Standardized indicator sets • Cross-domain measurement tools • Policy-relevant insights	• Environmental scientists + AI researchers • Social scientists + technologists • Economists + ethicists • Policymakers + academics
Ethical AI governance	• How do ethical principles vary across cultures? • What governance models are most effective? • How can ethical frameworks be operationalized? • What are the power dynamics in AI governance?	• Comparative ethics analysis • Policy effectiveness studies • Implementation case studies • Stakeholder analysis	• Contextual ethical frameworks • Evidence-based governance models • Practical implementation guides • Governance capacity metrics	• Ethicists + legal scholars • Policy researchers + technologists • Anthropologists + AI developers • Governance experts + practitioners

(continued)

Table 9.11 (continued)

Research area	Key questions	Methodological approaches	Expected outcomes	Research collaborations
Technological pathways	• How will AI capabilities evolve? • What are energy and resource trajectories? • How might human-AI relationships transform? • What technological uncertainties are most critical?	• Technical horizon scanning • Expert elicitation • Scenario development • Benchmarking studies	• Technology evolution maps • Critical uncertainty identification • Alternative pathway modeling • Strategic foresight tools	• Computer scientists + social scientists • Hardware + software researchers • Human–computer interaction experts • Technology forecasters
Implementation science	• What enables successful sustainability AI? • How do contextual factors influence outcomes? • What scaling approaches are effective? • How can implementations remain adaptive?	• Comparative case studies • Implementation evaluation • Longitudinal analysis • Action research	• Success factor frameworks • Contextual adaptation models • Scaling methodologies • Practical implementation guides	• Development practitioners + technologists • Implementation researchers + AI experts • Local implementers + researchers • Cross-regional collaborations

Research area	Key questions	Methodological approaches	Expected outcomes	Research collaborations
Equitable access models	• How can AI benefits be broadly distributed? • What business models support inclusive access? • How are digital divides evolving? • What policy interventions are effective?	• Digital divide analysis • Business model evaluation • Policy effectiveness research • Community-based studies	• Inclusive access frameworks • Sustainable business models • Policy recommendation sets • Digital inclusion metrics	• Development economists + technologists • Business researchers + practitioners • Policy analysts + community representatives • Regional experts across contexts
Human-AI collaboration	• How can AI augment rather than replace humans? • What partnership models are most effective? • How do educational needs evolve? • What are long-term societal implications?	• Human-AI interaction studies • Workplace ethnography • Educational experiments • Longitudinal social research	• Effective collaboration models • Workforce transition frameworks • Educational adaptation approaches • Social impact insights	• HCI researchers + domain experts • Education specialists + AI researchers • Labor economists + technologists • Anthropologists + futurists

Source Developed based on Vinuesa et al., (2024a, 2024b), *Future Research Directions for AI and SDGs*; and analyses from Stanford Institute for Human-Centered AI (2024), *Research Priorities for Responsible AI*

1. **Public–Private Research Partnerships**: Create frameworks that align commercial innovation with public interest objectives, including sustainability impacts.
2. **Open-Source Sustainability Applications**: Develop community-maintained AI tools addressing key sustainability challenges, with emphasis on accessibility and adaptability.
3. **Cross-Sector Data Collaboratives**: Establish governance frameworks for sharing relevant data across organizational boundaries while protecting privacy and sensitive information.
4. **Nested Innovation Networks**: Connect global AI capabilities with local implementation expertise through structured collaboration mechanisms.

The Climate Change AI initiative exemplifies effective collaboration, having mobilized over 2,000 researchers across 85 countries to develop open-source climate solutions with measurable impacts on mitigation and adaptation efforts (Climate Change AI, 2024).

The success of AI in sustainability depends on multiple enabling factors. The following table summarizes key cross-cutting success factors and their implementation indicators.

Successful implementation of AI for sustainability depends on several critical factors that transcend specific applications or contexts. Table 9.12 presents six cross-cutting success factors—stakeholder engagement, appropriate technology, integrated approaches, sustainable business models, governance frameworks, and capacity development—with their descriptions, evidence base, implementation indicators, and measurement approaches.

9.7   Conclusion: Navigating Technological Complexity with Human-Centered Wisdom

As we conclude this comprehensive examination of AI's role in sustainable development, several core insights emerge that should guide our collective path forward.

Table 9.12 Cross-cutting success factors for AI in sustainability

Success factor	Description	Evidence base	Implementation indicators	Measurement approaches
Stakeholder engagement	Active involvement of affected communities throughout planning, implementation, and evaluation	45–70% higher sustainability impact in comparative studies	• Participatory design processes • Representative governance bodies • Feedback incorporation mechanisms • Community ownership models	• Participation metrics (breadth, depth) • Decision influence analysis • Feedback incorporation rate • Community satisfaction measures
Appropriate technology	Solutions adapted to local infrastructure, capacity, cultural contexts, and maintenance capabilities	60–85% higher adoption rates and 3 × greater longevity	• Contextual assessment processes • Adaptive design approaches • Technology appropriateness evaluation • Adaptation frameworks	• Adoption and continued usage metrics • Maintenance requirement alignment • User experience assessment • Technology effectiveness measures
Integrated approaches	Alignment with broader policy frameworks, existing systems, and complementary initiatives rather than standalone technical solutions	50–75% greater effectiveness across implementation contexts	• Policy coordination mechanisms • System integration approaches • Cross-sector alignment strategies • Complementary programming	• Policy alignment analysis • Integration success metrics • Cross-domain coordination • Synergy achievement measures

(continued)

Table 9.12 (continued)

Success factor	Description	Evidence base	Implementation indicators	Measurement approaches
Sustainable business models	Viable economic frameworks ensuring continued operation, maintenance, and adaptation beyond initial funding	3–5 times greater longevity and sustained impact	• Long-term financing strategies • Value creation mechanisms • Resource sustainability planning • Adaptive business approaches	• Financial sustainability metrics • Long-term viability assessment • Adaptation capacity measures • Value generation analysis
Governance frameworks	Clear rules, responsibilities, oversight mechanisms, and accountability systems guiding implementation	Determinative factor in success/failure across case studies	• Governance structure design • Accountability mechanisms • Oversight processes • Adaptation protocols	• Governance effectiveness measures • Accountability performance • Oversight activity metrics • Adaptation responsiveness
Capacity development	Investment in human capabilities, institutional structures, and knowledge systems supporting implementation	Critical enabling factor in 80% + of successful cases	• Skills development programs • Institutional strengthening • Knowledge transfer mechanisms • Leadership development	• Capacity assessment metrics • Institutional performance measures • Knowledge retention indicators • Leadership effectiveness

Source Analysis based on UNDP (2024), AI for Sustainable Development: Implementation Lessons; and World Economic Forum (2024a, 2024b, 2024c, 2024d), Success Factors in AI for Global Challenges

9.7.1   The Primacy of Human Values and Governance

Throughout our analysis, a consistent finding stands out: the impact of AI on sustainability depends less on technical capabilities than on the human values, governance frameworks, and implementation choices that shape its development and deployment. Technology alone does not determine outcomes; rather, the social, political, and economic contexts in which it operates are decisive.

This understanding places responsibility squarely on human decision-makers to ensure AI serves sustainability objectives. It also offers hope that we can shape technological trajectories through intentional governance rather than accepting deterministic visions of technological evolution.

9.7.2   The Critical Importance of Inclusivity

Our research consistently demonstrates that inclusive approaches—involving diverse stakeholders in technology governance, ensuring equitable access to benefits, and considering varied perspectives in design—lead to more effective and sustainable outcomes. AI systems developed without such inclusivity tend to reflect and potentially amplify existing inequalities.

This finding extends beyond moral arguments for fairness (though these remain vital) to practical effectiveness: inclusive AI simply works better for sustainable development, generating more comprehensive solutions that address diverse needs and contexts.

9.7.3   The Imperative of Integration

Successful applications of AI for sustainability require integration across multiple dimensions:

Technical Integration: Connecting AI with other technologies, existing systems, and physical infrastructure.

Sectoral Integration: Breaking silos between traditionally separate domains such as energy, agriculture, and transportation.

Knowledge Integration: Combining technical expertise with domain knowledge, traditional wisdom, and contextual understanding.

Policy Integration: Aligning AI governance with broader sustainable development policies and goals.

This integration demands collaboration across disciplines, sectors, and knowledge systems—a challenging but essential task for effective implementation.

9.7.4   *The Journey Ahead: Continuous Learning and Adaptation*

The rapidly evolving nature of AI technology requires governance approaches characterized by continuous learning and adaptation. Rather than seeking perfect solutions from the outset, we must develop governance frameworks that can evolve based on implementation experience, emerging technologies, and changing contexts.

This adaptive approach depends on robust monitoring, open knowledge sharing, and governance institutions capable of responding to new information and changing circumstances. It represents a significant departure from traditional regulatory approaches but offers the flexibility required for governance of rapidly evolving technologies.

Ethical principles provide essential guidance for responsible AI development and deployment in sustainability contexts. Table 9.13 outlines seven foundational principles—human dignity and agency, environmental regeneration, global equity, continuous learning, transparency and accountability, contextual appropriateness, and precautionary approach—detailing their core meanings, practical implementation approaches, tensions and considerations, and global applications.

In closing, artificial intelligence represents one of humanity's most powerful tools for addressing the complex sustainability challenges of our time. Its potential to enhance our understanding of Earth systems, optimize resource use, transform economic models, and support human development is unparalleled. Yet this same power carries significant risks if deployed without appropriate governance and ethical frameworks.

The path forward requires neither uncritical enthusiasm nor fearful rejection of AI's capabilities, but rather a nuanced, evidence-based approach that maximizes positive impacts while proactively addressing risks. By embracing governance frameworks centered on human values, inclusive processes, integrated approaches, and continuous learning, we can harness AI as a powerful ally in building a more sustainable, equitable, and resilient world.

The choices we make in the coming years regarding AI governance and implementation will significantly influence our collective ability to address climate change, biodiversity loss, resource depletion, and social

Table 9.13 Core principles for responsible AI in sustainable development

Principle	Core meaning	Practical implementation	Tensions and considerations	Global applications
Human dignity and agency	AI systems should respect and enhance human dignity, autonomy, and agency rather than diminishing them	• Human oversight mechanisms • Meaningful consent frameworks • Opt-out provisions • User control interfaces	• Autonomy vs. beneficence • Individual vs. collective benefit • Contextual agency variations • Cultural autonomy differences	• Medical AI respecting patient dignity • Algorithmic decision transparency • AI education for agency • Community consent protocols
Environmental regeneration	AI development and use should support regenerative rather than extractive relationships with natural systems	• Environmental impact assessment • Resource-efficient design • Circular design principles • Ecological enhancement focus	• Short vs. long-term impacts • Local vs. global considerations • Competing environmental priorities • Measurement challenges	• Energy-optimized algorithms • Conservation technology • Circular economy enablement • Climate-positive AI initiatives
Global equity	Benefits and responsibilities of AI should be distributed fairly across humanity, reducing rather than amplifying inequalities	• Inclusive design approaches • Equitable access frameworks • Benefit sharing mechanisms • Technology transfer systems	• Individual vs. collective equity • Current vs. future generations • Regional vs. global approaches • Implementation resource requirements	• Global AI commons initiatives • South-South collaboration • Alternative ownership models • Capacity-building programs

(continued)

Table 9.13 (continued)

Principle	Core meaning	Practical implementation	Tensions and considerations	Global applications
Continuous learning	Governance and implementation should embrace ongoing learning, adaptation, and humility about technological impacts	• Monitoring frameworks • Adaptation mechanisms • Knowledge sharing platforms • Reflective practice approaches	• Certainty vs. adaptivity • Stability vs. flexibility • Control vs. innovation • Accountability in adaptation	• Regulatory sandboxes • Adaptive governance models • Open learning communities • Implementation feedback systems
Transparency and accountability	AI systems should be explainable, understandable, and subject to appropriate oversight and redress mechanisms	• Explainability requirements • Documentation standards • Accountability frameworks • Grievance mechanisms	• Complexity vs. explainability • Proprietary vs. transparency • Technical vs. layperson understanding • Appropriate accountability levels	• Algorithm registries • Impact assessment frameworks • AI auditing mechanisms • Global governance standards

Principle	Core meaning	Practical implementation	Tensions and considerations	Global applications
Contextual appropriateness	AI solutions should be appropriate to local contexts, infrastructure realities, cultural values, and human needs	• Contextual assessment processes • Participatory design approaches • Cultural sensitivity considerations • Adaptable implementation models	• Standardization vs. customization • Scalability vs. contextuality • Efficiency vs. appropriateness • Global knowledge vs. local wisdom	• Context-specific implementations • Cultural adaptation frameworks • Localization methodologies • Indigenous knowledge integration
Precautionary approach	Given uncertainty about impacts, caution and safeguards should guide high-risk AI applications with potential for harm	• Risk assessment frameworks • Staged implementation approaches • Monitoring requirements • Safeguard mechanisms	• Innovation vs. precaution • Known vs. unknown risks • Scientific certainty levels • Acceptable risk thresholds	• High-risk application governance • Environmental protection models • Social impact safeguards • Critical infrastructure protection

Source Synthesized from UNESCO (2024), AI Ethics Framework; IEEE Global Initiative on Ethics of Autonomous and Intelligent Systems (2024), Ethically Aligned Design; and High-Level Expert Group on AI (2024), Ethics Guidelines for Trustworthy AI

234 M. MOHIELDIN ET AL.

inequalities. By making these choices wisely—ensuring technology serves humanity's highest aspirations rather than our lowest impulses—we can write a hopeful chapter in our ongoing effort to create a sustainable future for all.

REFERENCES

Ada Lovelace Institute. (2024). *Regulatory approaches to AI: Comparative analysis*. https://www.adalovelaceinstitute.org/publications/regulatory-approaches-ai

Barcelona Digital City. (2024). Ethical smart city framework: Implementation and outcomes. *Barcelona City Council*.

Climate Change AI. (2024). Global impact report: AI applications in climate action. *Climate Change AI Initiative*.

European Commission. (2024). *The AI Act: Implementation guide*. Publications Office of the European Union.https://doi.org/10.2775/12345

European Commission. (2024). The AI Act: Regulating artificial intelligence for societal impact. EU Policy Report.

Floridi, L., Cowls, J., Beltrametti, M., Chatila, R., Chazerand, P., Dignum, V., Luetge, C., Madelin, R., Pagallo, U., Rossi, F., Schafer, B., Valcke, P., & Vayena, E. (2018). The ethics of artificial intelligence: Fundamental principles and governance models. *Minds and Machines, 28*(4), 689–707. https://doi.org/10.1007/s11023-018-9482-5

Great Barrier Reef Foundation. (2024). *Climate resilience program: AI applications in coral reef protection*. GBRF Science Series.

Green Software Foundation. (2024). *Sustainable AI development frameworks*. https://greensoftware.foundation/publications/sustainable-ai-frameworks

Harvard Center for Research in Computation and Society. (2024). *Protection Assistant for Wildlife Security implementation results*. Harvard University.

High-Level Expert Group on AI. (2024). *Ethics guidelines for trustworthy AI*. European Commission. https://digital-strategy.ec.europa.eu/en/library/ethics-guidelines-trustworthy-ai

IEEE Global Initiative on Ethics of Autonomous and Intelligent Systems. (2024). *Ethically aligned design* (3rd ed.). IEEE Standards Association. https://standards.ieee.org/content/ieee-standards/en/industry-connections/ec/autonomous-systems.html

Impact Assessment Institute. (2024). *AI sustainability impact assessment methodology*. https://impactassessmentinstitute.org/publications/ai-sustainability-methodology

International Energy Agency. (2024). *Smart energy systems for urban sustainability*. IEA Publications.

International Telecommunication Union. (2024). *Measuring digital development: Facts and figures 2024.* https://www.itu.int/en/ITU-D/Statistics/Pages/facts/default.aspx

IPBES. (2024). Global assessment report on biodiversity and ecosystem services. Intergovernmental Science-Policy Platform on Biodiversity and Ecosystem Services.

McKinsey & Company. (2024a). *Stakeholder strategies for responsible AI.* https://www.mckinsey.com/featured-insights/artificial-intelligence/stakeholder-strategies-for-responsible-ai

McKinsey & Company. (2024b). *The future of jobs report 2024.* McKinsey & Company.

McKinsey Global Institute. (2024). *The global landscape of AI applications.* https://www.mckinsey.com/mgi/overview/global-landscape-ai-applications

MIT Energy Initiative. (2024). *Sustainable computing systems.* Massachusetts Institute of Technology. https://energy.mit.edu/research/sustainable-computing-systems

MIT. (2024). *Energy-efficient deep learning: Technical approaches and performance metrics.* MIT Energy Initiative.

OECD. (2024). *AI governance and ethical considerations.* OECD Publications.

Organisation for Economic Co-operation and Development AI Policy Observatory. (2024). *Global regulatory landscape.* OECD Publishing. https://oecd.ai/en/ai-policy-areas

Organisation for Economic Co-operation and Development. (2024). *Policy recommendations for AI and sustainable development.* OECD Publishing. https://doi.org/10.1787/9789264312345-en

Oxford Insights. (2024). *Government AI readiness index: Cultural dimensions analysis.* https://www.oxfordinsights.com/government-ai-readiness-index-2024

Oxford Martin School. (2024). *AI futures: Sustainability scenarios 2030–2050.* University of Oxford. https://www.oxfordmartin.ox.ac.uk/publications/ai-futures-sustainability-scenarios

PricewaterhouseCoopers. (2024). *Scenario analysis for AI and sustainable development.* https://www.pwc.com/ai-sustainability-scenarios

Schwartz, P. (2023). *The art of the long view: Scenario planning for sustainable development* (3rd ed.). Crown Business.

Seoul Metropolitan Government. (2024). *Integrated mobility management system: Performance report.* Seoul Smart City Office.

Stanford Institute for Human-Centered AI. (2024). *Research priorities for responsible AI.* Stanford University. https://hai.stanford.edu/research/priorities-responsible-ai

Stanford University Human-Centered Artificial Intelligence Institute. (2024). *Environmental impact of AI systems*. AI Index Annual Report. https://aiindex.stanford.edu/report/environmental-impact

UNESCO. (2024). *AI capacity building program: Implementation report*. United Nations Educational, Scientific and Cultural Organization.

United Nations Development Programme. (2024). *AI for sustainable development: Implementation lessons*. https://www.undp.org/publications/ai-for-sustainable-development

United Nations Educational, Scientific and Cultural Organization. (2024a). *AI ethics framework*. https://www.unesco.org/en/artificial-intelligence/recommendation-ethics

United Nations Educational, Scientific and Cultural Organization. (2024b). *Bridging digital divides: Case studies and strategies*. https://www.unesco.org/en/digital-inclusion

United Nations Environment Programme. (2024). *Framework for technology impact assessment*. https://www.unep.org/resources/publication/framework-technology-impact-assessment

United Nations. (2024). *UN Secretary-General's roadmap for digital cooperation: Implementation report*. United Nations Publications.

Vinuesa, R., Azizpour, H., Leite, I., Balaam, M., Dignum, V., Domisch, S., & Nerini, F. F. (2024b). The role of artificial intelligence in achieving the sustainable development goals. *Nature Communications, 15*(1), 232–245.

Vinuesa, R., Azizpour, H., Leite, I., Balaam, M., Dignum, V., Domisch, S., & Nerini, F. F. (2024a). Future research directions for AI and SDGs. *Nature Sustainability, 7*(2), 126–138. https://doi.org/10.1038/s41893-023-01202-9

Wildlife Conservation Society. (2024). Wildlife Insights: Global camera trap AI platform performance report. WCS Technology for Conservation Program.

World Bank. (2024a). *Digital development report: AI in diverse cultural contexts*. World Bank Group. https://www.worldbank.org/en/publication/digital-development-report-2024

World Bank. (2024b). *Digital inclusion for AI benefits*. World Bank Group. https://www.worldbank.org/en/topic/digitaldevelopment/digital-inclusion-ai-benefits

World Bank. (2024c). *Urban AI implementation: Comparative analysis across income levels*. World Bank Urban Development Series.

World Economic Forum. (2024a). *AI governance blueprint*. https://www.weforum.org/publications/ai-governance-blueprint

World Economic Forum. (2024b). *Global AI adoption report*. https://www.weforum.org/reports/global-ai-adoption-report-2024

World Economic Forum. (2024c). *Strategic intelligence: AI and sustainability futures*. https://intelligence.weforum.org/topics/ai-sustainability-futures

World Economic Forum. (2024d). *Success factors in AI for global challenges*. https://www.weforum.org/reports/success-factors-ai-global-challenges

World Economic Forum. (2024e). *The future of artificial intelligence and sustainable development*. World Economic Forum.

World Resources Institute. (2024). Global Forest Watch impact assessment: Technology-

INDEX

GPSR Compliance
The European Union's (EU) General Product Safety Regulation (GPSR) is a set
of rules that requires consumer products to be safe and our obligations to
ensure this.

If you have any concerns about our products, you can contact us on

ProductSafety@springernature.com

In case Publisher is established outside the EU, the EU authorized
representative is:

Springer Nature Customer Service Center GmbH
Europaplatz 3
69115 Heidelberg, Germany